PARLIAMENTARY COMMITTEES:

ENHANCING DEMOCRATIC GOVERNANCE

Cavendish
Publishing
Limited

London • Sydney

PARLIAMENTARY COMMITTEES:

ENHANCING DEMOCRATIC GOVERNANCE

A Report of the Commonwealth Parliamentary Association
Study Group on Parliamentary Committees
and Committee Systems

Written and compiled by

Dr Gordon Barnhart

Cavendish
Publishing
Limited

London • Sydney

First published in Great Britain 1999 by Cavendish Publishing Limited,
The Glass House, Wharton Street, London WC1X 9PX, United Kingdom
Telephone: + 44 (0) 20 7278 8000 Facsimile: + 44 (0) 20 7278 8080
E-mail: info@cavendishpublishing.com
Visit our Home Page on http://www.cavendishpublishing.com

British Library Cataloguing in Publication Data.

Parliamentary committees: enhancing democratic governance in the commonwealth

1. Legislative bodies – Commonwealth countries – Committees
2. Representative government and representation – Commonwealth countries
3. Parliamentary practice – Commonwealth countries

I. Commonwealth Parliamentary Association

328.3′65′091712′41

ISBN 1 85941 532 6

Printed and bound in Great Britain

FOREWORD

When Commonwealth discussions on ways to strengthen democratic systems of government focus on the role of Parliament, the performance of its members or the involvement of the public in the decision making process, it is the clear consensus that all these areas can be enhanced through the work of parliamentary committees. In large Parliaments and small and in all regions of the Commonwealth, careful consideration is being given either to the expansion of committee work in those Houses with existing systems or to the introduction of deliberative and investigative committees in those Assemblies which have made limited use of references to small groups of their members. Committee systems are seen today as one of the most effective processes to make Parliament more responsive, members' roles more relevant and the democratic process more representative of, and accountable to, the views of the people.

Committees have been integral parts of the parliamentary process for nearly as long as there have been established procedures for the conduct of public business. Breaches of parliamentary privilege, the scrutiny of public accounts, reviews of legislation in detail and management decisions concerning the operation of the institution itself have long been referred to committees for less formal discussion than was possible in the parliamentary chamber. But, over the last two decades, there has been a movement toward the use of committees to examine public policy as well, to investigate and debate political issues and the performance of the executive in committee as well as in the full chamber. A body of practice has therefore been developing in Commonwealth Parliaments and legislatures which reflects the diversity of approaches and motivations which have guided these evolving systems in their various forms.

Recognizing that in this diversity of practice is a wealth of Commonwealth experience that would assist all Parliaments and legislatures as they consider how to respond to public and parliamentary demands for greater responsibility and openness, the Commonwealth Parliamentary Association (CPA) determined that a group of senior parliamentarians experienced in committee work should be brought together from all regions of the Commonwealth to compare committee practices and identify new directions for development so committee systems can make an even fuller contribution towards making Parliaments more representative, responsible and relevant. As an organization of more than 140 Parliaments and legislatures with a history of nine decades of promoting the advancement of parliamentary forms of government first in the British Empire and, since 1948, in the Commonwealth of Nations, the CPA was uniquely placed to launch such a comparative review. The Association's Executive Committee therefore agreed to fund what would be its seventh Study Group on aspects of parliamentary practice since 1978. The Group of senior members listed below gathered in late 1997 in London and, armed with their own experiences reinforced by a collection of authoritative background papers on committee practices from dozens of Commonwealth assemblies, began work on the report which is published here. The Study Group was joined by Dr Gordon Barnhart, the former Clerk of both the Saskatchewan Legislative Assembly and the Senate of Canada, who acted as rapporteur. With the able assistance of Ms Laura Cavendish, then our Acting Assistant Editor, Dr Barnhart distilled the London discussions into this comprehensive analysis of the state of committee systems in the Commonwealth. With that report, we also publish the background papers on committee issues submitted by the Study Group members, and assessments from most of them on how committee systems can continue to evolve.

The result is this exceptional insight into committee practice, and beyond that into democratic governance, which constitutes a substantial contribution to the further strengthening of committee systems and thereby to the enhancement of the performance and public perception of Parliaments.

Arthur R Donahoe, QC
Secretary General
Commonwealth Parliamentary Association

Members of the Study Group

Mr Jim Anderton, MP, New Zealand

Mr Heng Chiang Meng, MP, Singapore

Dr the Hon CT Kuruneri, MP, Zimbabwe

Mr Desmond Leakey, MP, Jamaica

Senator David MacGibbon, Australia

Mr Peter Milliken, MP, Canada

Mr Giles Radice, MP, United Kingdom

Shri Jaswant Singh, MP, India

Rapporteur: Dr Gordon Barnhart, Canada

Assisted by: Ms Laura Cavendish, CPA Acting Assistant Editor

CONTENTS

CHAPTER 1

INTRODUCTION

In the last 20 years, the Commonwealth Parliamentary Association has organized six study groups of members of Commonwealth Parliaments to discuss various topics of interest and importance and in most cases, reports or books have been the outcome of these study groups. Topics covered by these study groups are: Parliament and Public Finance; Parliament and Science Policy; the Role of Second Chambers; the Security of Small States; Electoral Law and Practice; and Conflict of Interest Legislation. In 1992, it was agreed by a CPA Working Party that these study group reports were valuable to parliamentarians as they seek to improve the functioning of their own Parliaments.

In February 1995, the CPA Wilton Park Conference on 'Parliament and People: Making Democratic Institutions more Representative, Responsible and Relevant' produced a report of its findings which also has become an important reference book for the students of Parliament.

It is with this background of successful and important study group reports that the Executive Committee of the CPA, when it met in Sri Lanka in October 1995, decided to establish another study group on the functioning of committees in Parliaments in the Commonwealth 'with a view to recommending ways in which strengthening committee systems can enhance the performance and public perception of Parliaments and parliamentarians'.

Dr Gordon Barnhart, Clerk Emeritus of the Legislative Assembly of Saskatchewan and of the Senate of Canada, was commissioned to act as the rapporteur for the study group. Ten topics were chosen for possible papers and eight parliamentarians from the various regions of CPA were invited to participate in this study group. These members, representing small and large, bicameral and unicameral Parliaments in countries with 'first-past-the-post' system of elections and systems of proportional representation, prepared papers on the various topics based on their own vast experience. Even though the members came from different cultures and political histories, and even different systems of government, they shared a common history of being members of the Commonwealth and part of the heritage of the Westminster model of Parliament. Notwithstanding their differences, they found that they shared many themes in common.

The study group met in London in early September 1997 to discuss and even debate the papers that had been prepared in advance. Every member shared his own experiences and knowledge. This book is a compilation of these opinions, and strongly held points of view. All members prepared a paper on the 'Future of the Committee System'. In addition to the material prepared and presented by the eight members, parliamentarians and Table Officers from all other Parliaments within the CPA were invited to prepare papers on any of the selected topics so as to have the experiences from the widest possible sources of information and experience.

The study group worked well together and it is hoped that this report will be useful to future students of Parliament and to present practitioners of the art of politics throughout the Commonwealth.

The Wilton Park Conference looked at ways that Parliament could become more representative, responsible and relevant. The overall theme of the study group on committees was similar in that these three "r's" could also apply to the committees of Parliament. In a time when Parliament seems to be under increased scrutiny and the object of cynicism, it is important to look at the principles of public life as outlined by the United Kingdom Committee on Standards in Public Life, chaired by Lord Nolan. This committee outlined several principles that elected officials should follow to be respected leaders in public life: selflessness; integrity; objectivity; accountability; openness; honesty; and leadership.

The study group followed several themes in its examination of the committee systems throughout the Commonwealth. The group noted that in Parliament and especially at the committee level, there is a constant struggle by the Private Members to hold the executive accountable. Are committees the way that members can check the powers of the executive branch of government or are the committees merely 'make work' programmes for Private Members without actual effect on the public policy? Do committees fill a need within the Parliament or have they become archaic in a time when decisions must be made on very short notice? Do the current executives actually listen to debate in committees and follow their advice? Do the members of the committees have adequate access to information and research services to be well prepared for committee debates and examinations or are they expected to ratify government initiatives with little debate or review? Do committee members have the proper tools, both in information and technically such as computers and the internet, to compete with a well supplied executive? Are the committees an avenue for the public to speak to the Parliament or are they sources of frustration for the public who complain that no one is listening? These are some of the themes that the study group wrestled with as they looked at Commonwealth committees from various angles.

It has been suggested that committees are a venue where members can toss aside their partisan beliefs and work as a non-partisan group in honestly listening to the public will and reviewing government initiatives and programmes. Is this possible in the real world? Are there any jurisdictions where the government has willingly relaxed the pressure on members to vote along party lines, even in committee? Members are torn between representing the will of their constituents and voting with their parties to maintain a majority or just even the party line. Has the power or the strength of the political parties increased over time to the detriment of the Private Member and, some would argue, the detriment of Parliament itself? At a time when cynicism toward Parliament and parliamentarians seems to be at an all time high, was there ever a 'golden age' for Parliament when members were free to vote consistently on conscience and in tune with the majority wishes of their constituents? If there was this golden age, is it possible to return to it? Are the committees the place where members can start the restoration of the rights and role of Private Members in holding government accountable? These are all questions that the study group wrestled with in assessing the role of committees in Parliament and in seeking some 'positive solutions' for members of the CPA.

It is widely recognized throughout the Commonwealth that the executive's role within the system of government has increased as the public expectation has demanded that government become more involved in daily living from education to road building and from health care to regulation of health and safety standards. This increased size of the government's mandate has led to an increase in the size of the public service and the overall annual expenditure of public funds. Governments in many Commonwealth countries have been willing to build new office towers and equip offices with the latest equipment to provide a requested and needed service to the public. On the other hand, governments have been less willing to invest tax dollars into an effective parliamentary system which would only become an obstacle to 'effective and efficient' government. Within government circles, it is common for ministers to believe that members of Parliament are obstacles to the efficient flow of decision making. Public servants are often heard to complain that the debates in the House or in committee are a 'waste of time'. It is rare for any government to encourage the strengthening of Parliament as a way of encouraging honesty in government or responsiveness to the public will. Governments have tended to grow in size and expenditure at a faster rate than Parliaments have experienced. Yet, if the Parliament is to hold the government accountable, it must have the staff, equipment and time to question ministers and senior public servants. Public involvement in decision making is often discouraged by government, especially if the consensus of this public opinion is opposed to government policy.

At a time when government's expenditures have increased, there has also been a trend for Parliament, especially in committee, to abandon the practice of reviewing detailed budget estimates before the passage of the government's annual budget. This principle of 'grievance before supply' has been forgotten. When estimates were being reviewed annually, the government's record of expenditure over the past year was also up for review. Government is particularly vulnerable when waiting for Parliament to approve the annual budget. Once the annual expenditure plans have been passed, government is less likely to listen to Parliament's concerns. The committee structure may be an avenue to restore Parliament's role of holding government accountable.

In like manner, it has been argued that the power of the political party over the individual member has increased over the last few decades. Party discipline has been a factor in preventing government members from openly criticizing government policy. Committees in many jurisdictions have become sterile sessions where one group of members defends the government on all issues while the opposition are the only group to offer alternatives or to criticize the government.

To have a system of government that is effective and efficient in setting public policy and administering public programmes, it is necessary to have a government strong enough to hold a majority or at least a coalition of supporters to pass their measures through Parliament. On the other hand, the system of government must have a means of listening to public complaints and have a review at the polls at least once every five years of the government's past practices and future plans. This is a fine balance between having a government strong enough to govern yet sensitive to the public will and opposition voices. Perhaps committees can assist Parliament in restoring its public image and ensure that government is more sensitive to the public will.

The study group looked at four types of committees: legislative, financial, administrative and postmortem review committees. Each type of committee serves a different yet essential need within a Parliament.

The group also looked at the media's role in setting public expectation of Parliament. Political leaders around the world have come under closer scrutiny by the media not only for their public actions and beliefs but also their actions in their own personal lives. Perhaps the life styles of leaders have not changed much over the years but the public scrutiny of their personal lives has increased. This has led to an increase in public cynicism about public officials and politics generally. The media has also publicized the role of committees within the American congressional model where committees tend to be more independent of the House and more powerful in their examinations. Television coverage of American committee hearings has distributed more knowledge about the American system but little about the differences with the Westminster style of Parliament. The public has sometimes failed to realize the differences between a presidential and a parliamentary form of government and has expected the Commonwealth committees to function in a similar manner to the American committees.

Television and radio, at the same time, have offered the public a greater opportunity to become more involved in the setting of public policy. More people are now able to watch or listen to the parliamentary debates and to influence government through either representation before a committee or demonstrations in the streets. The media have played a role in enabling pressure groups to exert an influence on the government. In like manner, pressure groups or lobbies have increased in number and activity in an attempt to influence public policy. Again, the committee system can offer a medium between these public groups and the government.

As we approach the 21st century, the quest for information and the need to digest the flow of information has become crucial. For some regimes, public access to information has been refused with the result that the people are forced to vote on issues or for political parties without full knowledge of the situation. In like manner, if members of Parliament do not have all the information, they are unable to hold the government accountable.

Too much information can also be a problem. With the computer and the internet, there seems to be no limit on the amount of information that is available. The problem then becomes how can members sort and digest the vital pieces of information to make themselves aware of the issues and to question ministers. Members no longer can expect to keep up to date on all issues and must rely more and more on researchers and support personnel to be able to speak in the House and in committees. Often, there is not enough time for members to research issues or to debate them and priorities must be set. Committees can help a Parliament divide up the work so that more can be done within strict time frames. This requires the members to be well equipped for the task. It has been argued that committees steal the thunder or the limelight from the House and thus should be curbed for the protection of the power and status of the House. Perhaps it can be countered that committees can add to the respect given to Parliament and can create an atmosphere of greater efficiency and effectiveness.

Not only has our technological society created an information explosion but also decisions now must be made faster than ever before. With e-mail, facsimiles, television, and cellular telephones, events in one part of the world affect the rest of the globe instantaneously. Governments are being forced to make decisions at a much faster pace than ever before. This raises the argument that Parliament is too slow and not responsive enough to the demands placed on it by this fast-paced society. Should Parliament always be involved in decisions over wars, troop deployment, national emergencies or rapidly changing economies or is this the sole realm of the executive? Perhaps committees can be the medium for rapid responses to public issues and advice to the government within tight time frames.

One of the criticisms of Parliament is that people do not know what it is doing and do not understand the procedural, ceremonial, and historical image of Parliament. Many have called for more public education programs to make the citizens aware of the role of a Parliament and the reason for its procedures and ceremony. Again, perhaps committees can serve a role in putting the Parliament in touch with its most important clients – the public.

This study was established to address these issues through an assessment of the committee structure in Commonwealth Parliaments. The study group decided not to make recommendations for improvements in committee structures and procedures but instead to offer some 'positive options'. Each Parliament is different due to its size and political culture. Each Parliament is a reflection of its own country and has adapted procedures and structures that best suit the needs of its citizens. By outlining some positive options, Parliaments around the Commonwealth can pick and choose those applicable to their own needs. Each country must pick its own model Parliament and committee structure based on commonly accepted solutions that have worked in other Parliaments. It is hoped that this report will help Parliaments reassess their own committee procedures and structures and implement changes for the betterment of each Parliament.

CHAPTER 2

PURPOSE, FUNCTION AND OPERATION OF COMMITTEES

The National Democratic Institute (NDI) in the United States described the ideal committee in 'almost all democratic legislatures' as being composed of a smaller group of members designated to do the detailed work of the House.[1] The committee offers a less formal, less partisan atmosphere in which members can consider estimates or legislation with less control from the executive arm of government. Committees, if functioning in the ideal state, can be the focus of public input and the pipeline between the constituents and the government. This worldwide view is also applicable to the Westminster committee model.

The members of the study group found that committees in their Parliaments were considerably less than the ideal outlined by NDI but many predicted that reform was on the horizon. Committees could be reformed and restructured to become more efficient and effective. As Giles Radice (member of the House of Commons of the United Kingdom) noted, committees are not an end in themselves but a means to greater surveillance of government activity and policy:

> The present committee system has for the most part developed in response to the need to relieve the pressure of business on the Floor of the House or in response to new obligations or to demands for the House to perform new functions involving detailed investigation which are unsuited to a large assembly. The system which we have inherited is unplanned and unstructured.[2]

Even though the committee structure has had a relatively long history, there has not been a consistent evolution. Instead, the 'committee system has been one of evolution by fits and starts, rather than by steady progress'.[3]

It should also be noted that committees vary from country to country even within the Commonwealth:

> Parliamentary institutions tend to be rooted in the cultural identity of the populace as much as in the particular constitutional, statutory and procedural instruments which govern them ... The role of committees is a key indicator of the extent to which legislation is crafted and influenced by the elected representatives themselves.[4]

---

1 National Democratic Institute For International Affairs, 'Committees in legislatures: a division of labor', Legislative Research Series, paper 2, p 1.

2 First Report from the Select Committee on Procedure, HC (1977–78) 588, para 1.12.

3 Radice, G, 'The History of the Committee System on the Westminster Model', see p 161.

4 Paper prepared by the National Assembly of Pakistan, p 1.

Committees should not be mini chambers but instead, small working groups of members working informally together toward a common goal. This independent and informal atmosphere is dependent to a great extent on the power or influence of the political parties. If party discipline is rigid, the independence and often usefulness of a committee is severely reduced.

The role and function of the committee structure in any country is dependent on the role of political parties and the view the government has of the Parliament. The more powerful the political parties, the less influential the committees. Within the Westminster model, with the ever present struggle between the executive and legislative arms of government, the executive usually takes measures to prevent public embarrassment in committee. To accomplish this, the executive feels obliged to control the activities of the committee with its majority, thus reducing the nonpartisan level of debate within the committee. Executives are often compelled to limit the scope of enquiry of a committee and to influence the outcome of the committee investigation.

In contrast to the Parliamentary Committee's role and function, the American committees within the congressional model, appear to be much more independent of the executive and more in control of their own agendas. With the spread of American television programming and American movies around the world, the American model of government has become an example in the minds of many citizens, resulting in pressure being exerted on Commonwealth committee members to push for more power and control in their committees. A strict comparison between the congressional and parliamentary systems cannot be made, since in a congressional system, the executive is not a part of the legislative body. This fact alone changes the entire dynamic of power sharing within their system of government. In the American system, for example, the political party lines are less defined and the legislature has more independence in setting the agenda. However, balanced against this legislative power of initiation, the executive, in the form of the President, has the power of veto. Thus, it is through a system of checks and balances that the legislative power to initiate is tempered by the executive power of veto.

Within the Commonwealth or Westminster system of Parliament, the executive (Cabinet) sits within the legislative body and continues in power only as long as it can maintain a majority within the legislature. The members of the legislature have ready access to members of the executive, usually through a daily question period, but are restricted in their questions and criticism, at least in public, by the power of the majority party to control the behaviour of its own members. The threat of an election if the government is defeated is often enough to ensure all government members toe the party line. The Westminster model encourages members to vote along party lines which weakens the power of Parliament to hold the government accountable.

Private Members are not totally powerless. Often within the privacy of their own caucus, members are free to speak freely in representing their constituents and urging their parties to pursue a certain policy. Unfortunately, for these members, the public does not see the work done behind the scenes on their behalf. To show dissent against one's own party in public is not viewed with favour by the leadership and this can limit the member's chances for promotion within the party.

A government with a very large majority often can be even more unresponsive to the wishes of the members of Parliament. Large majorities often give the impression of a 'steam roller' and are unaffected by the minority voice. On the other hand, a close majority or even a minority government is often more sensitive to the requests of the minority in order to maintain the coalition or to hold on to power. Compromise is often the order of the day in a minority government. The government party must accommodate the wishes of the minority in order to stay in power. Procedures within committees are directly affected by the struggle of the executive to stay in power. Strict party discipline limits the scope and freedom of the committees to pursue certain investigations or to be critical of government policy.

With the Westminster model, members of a government are often lured by the desire to become part of the Cabinet where the decisions are made and the power is centralized. Private Members on the government side are thus tempted to toe the party line to draw favourable response from the Prime Minister and to be invited into Cabinet. Members may even try to become chairs of committees in order to attract the eye of the Prime Minister but this hardly leads to independent reviews by the committee. Large majorities and strong party discipline give the impression of stable government. What the majority has decided will become law. Even though governments with large majorities tend to stifle legislative independence and restrict the free flow of ideas from the population to the government by way of the Parliament, committees are useful as a way of keeping members busy. However, the temptation for government is to try to control or restrict the criticism coming from the committees. Strong and independent committees can lead to stronger and more responsive governments but it is rare for a government to take such a long term view. Governments usually react negatively to independent-minded committees and use their majority to limit such exhibits of independence by committees and their members.

Committees can ease the load on the House by doing detailed review of legislation or estimates but often do not use their time properly. Most of the time might be devoted to the first clause or two of a Bill and then the committee will pass the remainder of the Bill on the 'nod' due to the expiration of the allotted time. Time allocation is often used by government to ensure that their legislative agenda passes Parliament on time. This, however, limits the rights of the minority to delay a vote or passage of a Bill in order to draw a particular point to the attention of the public. The opposition must always have the right to delay public measures in an attempt to gain public support for their point of view. On the other hand, the public does not have much patience for 'senseless debate'. It is a rare ability within a political party to recognize the difference between constructive delay and unnecessary filibustering.

The powers of the committees are set, to a great extent, by the House. Committees are creatures of the House. In some jurisdictions, Parliaments have delegated to the committees the powers to set their own agendas and scope of inquiry. This can lead to more independence and publicly recognized members limited only by popular pressure. This comes back to the original point of the struggle between the executive and the legislative arms of government. If a government can take the long term view and delegate to the Parliament some independence and rely on the advice from the elected members with a minimum of party discipline, the government will be stronger. This though is not usually reflected in reality. Government by nature believes that it has the answer and is unwilling to take the risk of criticism coming from Parliament or its committees.

The media also plays a role in this struggle between executive and legislative arms of government. When there might be a very small division in the political ranks, or a member criticizes in committee the policy or platform of his/her own party, the media are quick to point this point out to the public, calling the member a 'renegade' or describing it as a crisis of confidence in the government. The matter may be minor but the media will often describe it as a confidence issue. The media's reaction to public criticism of government by its own members, even in committee, tends to discourage members from speaking out against their own government, thus limiting their independence and right to speak out on behalf of their constituents. Any member caught in the limelight due to criticism of their own government will likely never be chosen for leadership roles in the government. Banishment to the back benches for the remainder of their time in Parliament is the usual result. Members are encouraged, within the Westminster model, to express dissent within caucus but not publicly. This then limits the members' role in committee and in the House, lending credence to the popular belief that Private Members are there merely to vote along party lines without speaking out on issues that they enunciated during the last election. This, in turn, fuels the belief that politicians are not true to their word – they say one thing during an election and vote another way once elected. Members are rarely given credit for speaking out and changing public policy because this is done in closed caucus meetings or perhaps in camera meetings of a committee. In either case, the public is not aware of the representation made by the member which leads to further public cynicism directed at the parliamentary process and politics in general. More open committee meetings and a relaxation of party discipline will go a long way toward members being able to show the voting public that they can contribute to public policy and can represent the will of the constituents. This in turn would improve Parliament's credibility in the public's mind.

CHAPTER 3

TYPES OF COMMITTEES

Throughout the Commonwealth, the committee structures have evolved in different ways and have been given a variety of names. This chapter will try to capture a common theme on the types of committees that do exist and ways that perhaps committees can be strengthened.

The Committee of the Whole is a common committee in all Parliaments. Traditionally, the Committee of the Whole, made up of all members sitting usually in the legislative chamber, reviewed all proposed legislation and estimates. As Houses increased in size and sat for longer periods of time within the year, many Parliaments found that they had to delegate some of their work to smaller committees which met outside the chamber. This allowed more than one committee to meet at one time and often for smaller committees to meet simultaneously with the House. In some smaller Parliaments, where members are able to complete the nation's business well within a calendar year, there is less pressure to delegate work to smaller committees.

There are some advantages to having the work done in the Committee of the Whole. The moment that a matter is referred to a a smaller committee meeting in a room which is not as central as the chamber, there is a greater likelihood that the committee's proceedings will be ignored by the media and as a consequence by the public as well. The opposition can certainly hold the government minister accountable more effectively in full public view in the chamber during review of the estimates than in a small committee. Simultaneous committee hearings can promote more efficient use of time but can also mean that some committee meetings are over shadowed by the House or other committee meetings. The call for smaller committees to promote efficiency is valid only when it is shown that the Parliament cannot finish its business within the calendar year. The full glare of the House can be more effective for opposition parties and should not be sacrificed purely in the name of efficiency.

There is a great variety of nomenclature for the continuing Parliamentary Committees. In some jurisdictions, the continuing committees are called 'Standing Committees' while in others, they are 'Select Committees'. For the purposes of this chapter, the term 'Standing Committees' will be used to refer to committees that are established for the life of the Parliament and may have various matters sent to them. There are at least four types of Standing Committees:

(1) Legislative Committees. Some Parliaments have Standing Committees existing to review referred legislation while other Houses establish individual committees to review specific pieces of legislation. Reference to the committee may be before consideration of the principle of the Bill in the House or after approval of the principle. Even though the latter is the traditional procedure under the Westminster model, the Canadian House of Commons, for example, has begun to refer Bills to committee before adoption of the principle. The rationale for this change is to provide greater opportunity for members and the public to propose changes to the Bill before it becomes solidified and approved in principle. Once the principle has been approved by the House, the scope of possible amendment in committee is severely restricted. Criticism of this new procedure has been that the debate on the principle of the Bill is either eliminated or truncated which limits the opposition's right to a public debate on the merits of the Bill in the broad view. In the ideal, full review of the clauses of the Bill in committee followed by a broad debate in the House on the principle of the Bill would take advantage of both procedures. Governments complain, however, that this procedure would not 'speed up' the review process and thus oppose debate at both stages. The key element of the review by committee of legislation is to solicit public input and to hold the government accountable for its public policy and practices as well as its proposed legislative amendments.

(2) The second type of Standing Committee is the Financial Committee. This is a place for the members to review in some detail the departmental estimates of the government. It has been a trend throughout Commonwealth Parliaments that the estimates have not been reviewed thoroughly, if at all. Members have used their time to debate broad issues but have avoided detailed examinations of the estimates for several reasons. In order to undertake a detailed examination of the departmental estimates, the opposition member(s) must do much homework and must be well versed on the policies and past expenditures of that department in order to know what questions to ask. Members often do not have enough time to do this much preparation in advance. Secondly, members usually do not gain any press coverage from these reviews and procedurally do not have an opportunity to move amendments to the estimates. Within the Westminster model, members are limited to debating the estimates and are not allowed to move amendments to increase the budgeted allotment or to propose that the vote be reduced. To propose an increase is interpreted as a new charge on the public purse which involves a power and right reserved for ministers of the Crown. To move a reduction in the vote, the government usually defines as a motion of non-confidence and applies pressure on all government members to vote against the measure. As a result of the above two factors, members in most Parliaments have given up on trying to review government estimates, thus losing a once

effective tool in holding the government accountable. In addition, many public enterprises have been partially privatized in that they do not rely on an annual grant of funds from Parliament but are still part of the government. How can these companies or government ventures be reviewed by the parliamentary process?

One way to give members some motivation to review estimates would be to allow members to move motions to raise and lower departmental estimates without affecting the total money to be voted. This way, no new expenditures would be committed but members would have a way of proposing some valid reassignment of public funds. Governments would have to ease their definition of a 'non-confidence vote' in order to give members more freedom and motivation in reviewing estimates.

Committees can play a role in advising the Minister of Finance before the tabling of the annual budget. In the past, the budget was prepared by the minister and his/her officials in isolation and with a veil of strict secrecy. Ministers were sometimes forced to resign if the contents of the budget were 'leaked' before budget day. A more modern practice has developed in many Commonwealth countries whereby the Minister of Finance purposefully and publicly consults with the public in advance of tabling a budget. Parliamentary Committees can also be instructed to consult with the people and to seek input for the budget preparation process. The committee can be a means of two-way communication. The government can send out the word on how only certain expectations can be met and the public can advise the minister in a public way what their needs are and how they wish tax dollars to be spent. There are the usual three priorities: lower taxes; surpluses to be spent on new programmes; or surplus to be spent on lowering the public debt or deficit if the country still has one. Obviously, all three objectives cannot be met with lower taxes and greater expenditures and repayment of the debt. The public's opinion on the priorities to be met can be expressed through a Parliamentary Committee. It will then be up to the minister to determine the best course of action to take and defend his choices publicly. With the decline in the perceived need for budget secrecy, the public has a chance to influence financial policy in advance of the tabling of the annual budget.

(3) The third type of Standing Committee is the Administrative Committee, often known as a Board of Internal Economy or a Committee on Members' Services. This has been a relatively recent (within the last three decades) innovation in Commonwealth Parliaments. These Boards or Committees have members from government and opposition and usually have a majority of Private Members over cabinet ministers. These Administrative Committees review: human resource policies in the broad sense for all employees of the Parliament, and review the estimates for the operation of the House and its committees as well as for all expenses related to the

operation of the Parliament. In theory at least, this committee is to set policy and expenditure for the operation of the Parliament and its members and staff. The creation of Administrative Committees has increased Parliament's decision making power over the operation of its own proceedings without interference from the executive. These committees are usually chaired by the Speaker, again lending credence to the point that the House is master of its own fate and the Speaker is an independent arbiter on behalf of Parliament.

(4) The fourth type of committee is the 'Post-mortem' Review Committee such as the Public Accounts Committee or the Statutory Instruments Committee. These committees review accounts or regulations from the past year to ensure that the government has spent public funds wisely or has promulgated regulations within correct statutory authority. The purpose of these committees was obviously one more way to hold the government accountable. However, increasingly, it has become more difficult to attract members to these types of committees. Post-mortem Committees do not have 'press appeal' even though they do serve a useful purpose in holding the government accountable.

Some jurisdictions have Standing Committees whose purpose is to review past actions and expenditures of Crown corporations or public enterprises. Even though these corporations are at arm's length from government, this is a way of Parliament exercising a public review of the expenditure of public funds.

Special committees are appointed from time to time to undertake special and time limited reviews of subjects as identified by the House. Judicial inquiries or public commissions are appointed to do similar reviews but the special committee review has the advantage of involving elected members who have a closer view of the public will than a judge or a commissioner may have.

For bicameral Houses, the Joint Committee is another type of committee which is composed of members from both the upper and lower chambers. The mandate of a Joint Committee may be to review statutory instruments throughout the Parliament or it may be assigned a special review of a limited duration.

It can be argued that these various types of committees can improve the effectiveness and efficiency of Parliament. The terms effective and efficient are open to interpretation. In order to analyse a complex issue, a small group of members may be more effective as long as the membership has expertise in that particular field and the committee has access to specialized advisors. A committee is usually faced by a battery of governmental advisors who are experienced, well educated and armed with detailed information. A committee must have similar tools to achieve a proper review of the government's proposal.

Committees can be effective as a bridge between executive government and the public. Open public hearings and questioning of witnesses can inform members about the public will and alert them to important pending issues. It is true that a caucus committee made up of members from only one party can also hold hearings but their findings are not likely to be as reliable as a Parliamentary Committee report where people of all political persuasions come to speak to the committee.

Efficiency is often another measure of the committee's performance. Proponents of a strong committee system often claim that a committee is efficient when more bills are passed in a shorter time. But, is this necessarily an accurate measure of a committee's efficiency? The number of Bills that a Parliament passes in a year is only one measure of its productivity. Did the public have sufficient input into public policy? Were the measures not only in line with popular will but also 'good for the country?' Obviously, these measurements are relative. The true test of the efficiency and effectiveness of a government and the parliamentary process can be measured by the results of a general election; but it is hard to determine exactly which factors led to the defeat or reelection of a government. If committees have enabled the public to voice their concerns and have their suggestions heard, and if committees have assisted the members to consider the country's business within the year, both legislatively and financially, and if the government was held accountable for its actions, then a committee can claim with some measure of accuracy that they filled a useful role.

CHAPTER 4

SIZE OF COMMITTEES – SIZE OF HOUSE

Countries throughout the Commonwealth vary in geographic size and population. Accordingly, the size of the Parliaments vary considerably. It has been argued that, if a country has a small Parliament, there is no need for committees. The members can meet in the chamber and still be a relatively small working group. Smaller Houses tend to sit for shorter periods of time than larger Houses and thus have less need to save time by referring matters to committee. With a smaller membership, it is more difficult to establish committees because there are only so many members to fill all the spots. For all of the above reasons, one would assume that committees are not necessary and in fact are not advised for smaller Parliaments.

On the other hand, with smaller Parliaments, the executive tends to take up a larger proportion of the House. Committees with few or no ministers provide an opportunity for Private Members to contribute without the predominance of members of the executive.

In smaller legislatures, such as the one in Singapore, it is the custom not to challenge a minister in public. By custom, a Private Member would contradict or criticize a minister privately or in caucus. Smaller Parliaments in smaller communities tend to be more personal where everyone knows everyone else and there is a different dynamic than in a Parliament of over 200 members. This can be an advantage and a disadvantage. Smaller Parliaments tend to have closer contact with the voters and elected members may personally know every constituent. Committee consultations with the public may not be as necessary but still offer a vehicle for discussions.

With a smaller House, a problem may arise if there are not enough members to fill all of the committee posts. In any Parliament, there is usually a certain percentage of the members who are interested in serving on committees with the result that the members on the committees can be spread too thinly. This can result in a practice of substitution where one member replaces another with a resulting decline in consistency and knowledge of the subject before the committee. If members are appointed to too many committees, they will not have enough time to prepare adequately for the hearings.

Larger Parliaments can have similar problems in reverse. With members representing thousands if not hundreds of thousands of people, it is difficult for members to get to know their constituents and their needs. Committees can be useful in soliciting public input. Yet, if there are too many committees, scheduling problems arise.

It thus requires a careful balance to determine the correct size of committee structure to meet the needs and size of the individual country. Regardless of the country size, it is important to have committees to ease the workload on the House, to hear public representation and to discuss public issues in smaller groups. Expert witnesses can appear before a committee in a more informal manner than before the full House. Committees can be a way for a government to renew itself, to collect and implement new ideas and programs.

A frustration faced by most committee members within the Westminster model of Parliaments, no matter what the size of the country, its Parliament or its committees, is that there seems to be no way of 'forcing' the government to implement the recommendations in the committee report. Rules can be implemented requiring the government to respond, but such responses can be vague and irrelevant. The only way to press a government to respond is to rally public support for the committee report. If governments want to stay in power, they will respond if the public outcry is continuous and overwhelming. Co-operation amongst Private Members of both sides of the House and well researched and written reports can add pressure on government to respond. Careful media relations are a necessity in mounting pressure on the government. Regardless of the size of a country or its Parliament, governments in a freely elected system do respond to public pressure. Occasionally, government will adopt a policy that is not necessarily popular but is 'good for the country'. The government must, however, show the populace that the policy was sound before the next election or it will suffer the consequences.

CHAPTER 5

WITNESSES

In Australia, witnesses are vital to the operation of the Parliament and its committees. The committee proceedings are rarely adversarial or partisan and most meetings are open to the press and the public. For a committee to have enough information to counterbalance the artillery of public servants with thick briefing books, committees must call a wide variety of public experts. The citizen on the street who may not be an expert on that particular subject but has life experience and an opinion on the matter, is a logical committee witness. Being a taxpayer and voter, the opinion of the citizen is vital to an open democracy.

It is important to the parliamentary system that all witnesses tell the truth. In Canada, for example, perjury before a committee is a criminal offence. Witnesses, however, can face a dilemma. If they tell the truth, they may be incriminating themselves for a future court case. On the other hand, if they refuse to appear before a committee or refuse to answer the questions, they could be held in contempt of Parliament. A way around this dilemma is for committees to avoid examining potential criminal cases. These matters can be left to the courts. Another solution is found in Australia where evidence given before a committee is not admissible in a court.

Who then should be called before a committee? In theory, anyone can be called and, under order from Parliament, forced to appear. As with many things in life, there is a difference between theory and practice. Committees must be careful not to back themselves into a corner. If they call a minister or the Prime Minister and he/she refuses to appear, even though there may be public pressure for them to be there, the committee loses face if the witness fails to appear and the committee backs down. The atmosphere for calling public witnesses is usually more harmonious, often with a willingness on the part of the witness to appear before the committee.

The same may not be true for public servants. There can be a debate over who in the department is responsible: the minister or the top permanent public servant. If a public servant is called and appears before a Parliamentary Committee, it is likely that he/she compared notes with the minister first. However, if there is blame to be given out and if there were major problems within the department, must the public servant resign or is the minister responsible? There are varying practices throughout the Commonwealth on this point. The growing trend is that the minister will take responsibility for the problem and assure the House that the problem will be corrected. However, the minister is less likely to resign now than in the past. It is argued that with the increasing size of government, it is impossible for a minister to know everything that has happened in the department and, therefore, cannot be held personally responsible. In Canada, for example, ministers do not tend to resign for problems in their departments but do so if they are caught lying about the situation or are caught in a conflict of interest. In contrast, British ministers have resigned for not anticipating certain situations and have taken personal responsibility for the resulting problems.

The study group was agreed on the point that committees should not back themselves into a corner in insisting on calling witnesses when it appears that the person will not appear. Committees can usually accomplish their goals without confrontation or public embarrassment.

Committees must also use discretion in calling witnesses who are part of a vocal or a single-issue lobby group. Opinions expressed professionally by a lobby group with a vested interest have to be balanced with the testimony given by a citizen who has an interest in the subject but is not trained in public speaking and is not a professional lobbyist. It takes a skilled committee to be able to determine the difference between the voice of the general public and likely majority of the population versus the voice from the fringe minority. Witnesses can be a helpful tool to a committee in searching for as much information as possible and in trying to determine the truth.

CHAPTER 6

OCCUPANT OF THE CHAIR

Many governments around the Commonwealth are facing public cynicism as they form a majority in Parliament without having the support of the majority of the voters. With the 'first-past-the-post' voting system, governments are often formed without the support of over 50 per cent of the votes cast. Expressed another way, more than half of the people who voted expressed a preference for another party and, therefore, voted against the party that formed the government. New Zealand has adopted a new system which they hope will ensure that governments represent more than half of the votes cast. This new option is called the Mixed-Member Proportional system (MMP) which is a combination of 'first-past-the-post' and proportional representation which was adopted for a trial period by the people in a referendum in 1993. In its short history, no one party has been able to win a majority and thus it has been necessary to form a coalition of parties to govern. The Parliament has experienced some problems in implementing the new system where the government has tried to continue to manage the House by the old rules used in the first-past-the-post system. MMP is answering the complaint of governments not having the support of the majority of the people but there will have to be adjustments made to the parliamentary procedures.

One example of an adjustment in New Zealand is with the choice of chairpersons for the House and committees. Traditionally, the largest party has taken all of the posts for its own members and left itself in a position of controlling the operation of the Parliament. It is speculated that, in time, the government will have to share the chairs in order to win the support of smaller parties to form a coalition government.

Parliaments in other countries without MMP have adopted a system of sharing the posts of committee chair with the opposition. It is usual for the chair of the Public Accounts Committee, for example, to be occupied by an opposition member.

In New Zealand, MMP so far has created a situation of minority government which is having some positive effects on parliamentary procedures. It could be argued that this could have happened under the old system but under MMP, it is likely that no party will win a majority on its own and thus will have to be more amenable to compromise and coalition. Now that members of more than one party are needed to keep a government in power, their power as individuals in Parliament has increased. Private Members can group together on issues and defeat a cabinet minister if they so choose. The threat of this happening makes a cabinet more attentive to their supporters and ultimately to the Parliament itself. In like manner, if a Cabinet is less self-assured, committees become more relevant and exercise more influence. In New Zealand, committees are now making amendments to Bills over the objection of government. Cabinet is forced to accept the verdict of the committee because their own members have voted for the amendments. The question does arise, though: is it only the government members who are willing to break ranks or are opposition members equally as independent?

The study group was not willing to embrace the concept of MMP because of concerns over continual governmental instability and the inability of one party to form a government. On the other hand, they had to concede that MMP has brought change to the way the people of New Zealand practice politics. New Zealanders have yet to decide whether their experiment will continue and will be deemed a success.

Even though Canada has not adopted any form of proportional representation, procedures there have changed in the method that the occupants of the chair are chosen. In September 1986, the Canadian House of Commons changed its Standing Orders to allow a secret ballot election for the position of Speaker. Up to that point, the practice had been for the Prime Minister to nominate, seconded by the Leader of the Opposition, a member to be Speaker. The vote was an open voice vote and there were rarely any other candidates proposed for the post. Only in the case when a government did not have a majority in the House did the Prime Minister's choice suffer the chance of being overturned by the House. Notwithstanding the method of selection and the apparent close ties between the Prime Minister and the Speaker under the old system, the Canadian House of Commons over the years generally had good Speakers who tried to guide the House with an even hand. The implementation of a secret ballot in the election of Speaker has now meant that many candidates can stand for election as Speaker and all members have a say in choosing the person to take the chair. The perception and reality of having a Speaker chosen from the House rather than proposed by the Prime Minister has satisfied all members that the Speaker is their choice and has created a healthy distance between the government and the Speaker. The Canadian free vote system has yet to choose a candidate from the opposition. However, there are examples in both the United Kingdom and India where opposition members have been chosen as Speaker. A practice has been adopted in Canada, as well, of having some opposition members as Deputy Speaker, again lending some credence to the idea that the chair is to be neutral and fair to all members. The Canadian Speaker does not have a substantive vote but votes only in the case of a tie.

In contrast, the government of New Zealand still places its own members in the chair of the House and nearly all committees. The change here though is that the chair has a substantive vote and in the case of a tie the status quo is maintained.

Even though the concept of a free election for the occupant of the chair in the House is becoming widespread, there does not appear to be a move toward electing committee chairs by a free vote. Perhaps this is a future innovation for Commonwealth Parliaments.

In considering the post of Speaker or chair of a committee, is this post considered to be training ground for a 'promotion' to cabinet or a reward for someone who has had to leave cabinet earlier than desired? With more jurisdictions paying their Speakers more than the Private Members and in many cases as much as a cabinet minister, the financial advantage of going into cabinet is being eliminated. Although one never knows the details of the negotiations of who is invited into cabinet and why, it is rumoured that more Speakers are refusing the Prime Minister's invitation to join the cabinet and are choosing instead to remain in the chair. This phenomenon will only enhance the perceived independence of the occupant of the chair.

Even though the Speaker is expected to be neutral, is this the case for committee chairpersons as well? Is the chair most effective as a politically neutral person or as a leader of an inquiry? A good chairperson can be both. He/she can be neutral politically, refusing to favour one party over another, but yet can also lead an investigation with a goal of finding the truth even if it might be damaging to the government. The chances of an 'independent' chairperson ever being invited to sit in cabinet may be limited but the member knows that he/she played an important part in Parliament. A chairperson who was weak also does not necessarily have a better chance of cabinet unless the Premier is determined to surround him/herself with weak ministers. It is easy to suggest that a member should jeopardize his/her chances of 'promotion' by pursuing the role of 'freedom fighter'; but one can be idealistic about the merits of a good chair occupant.

There is growing debate over whether it is a 'promotion' to join cabinet. It is true that usually this involves more pay and more power but also has a price in time and responsibility. Only so many can ever achieve leadership roles in Parliament. Wise members use every opportunity they have to work in Parliament for the betterment of their jurisdiction and of their constituents. If this leads to offers for other ways to serve, so be it; but in the meantime, most members will seek to gain satisfaction in serving their constituents in the best manner possible.

CHAPTER 7

STAFF AND FACILITIES PROVIDED TO COMMITTEES

The study group considered four services that are or should be provided to committees to help the members fulfill their roles as parliamentarians. These services, ranked as top to bottom priorities, are: staff; open meetings; television and radio coverage of proceedings; and committee travel. Some Commonwealth countries have committee systems but do not provide their members with trained support staff. Members, often untrained and unable to understand the complexities of government accounting and reporting, are unable to offer constructive criticism of government policy or practice. These same Parliaments do not have adequate parliamentary libraries or research facilities where members can go to prepare for upcoming debates or consideration of legislation and estimates.

On the other extreme, some Parliaments provide their members with committee staff to keep the records, arrange witnesses, advise members on procedure and to prepare research papers and possible questions for the committee members. Furthermore, these Parliaments have well stocked research centres and libraries with a core of professional researchers who are available to members and who will write specific research papers on request. Committees also may have a budget to hire outside experts who can advise members on the issues before the committee and may be permitted to ask questions of government officials before the committee. Pushed to the extreme, this can lead to members being left on the sidelines watching a duel between two teams of hired experts.

Is there such a thing as too many services for members? Members of the study group felt that it is better to have too much rather than not enough. The problem arises though that as members get very busy, they often do not have time to read the briefing books that were prepared by researchers. If a member is on too many committees or has been named to a committee as a substitute at the last moment, he or she will not have sufficient time to prepare. Yet it is important that members be given the tools to adequately question the minister or the departmental officials. Since governments usually have the resources to hire their own experts, they have an advantage over the parliamentary members who are lacking the research capabilities and resources to adequately prepare. These research facilities do represent a cost to the public purse, but it is argued that this is a necessary expenditure to ensure that the Parliament is giving the government full scrutiny and holding the executive accountable. Staff to the committees may also help draft committee reports for consideration by the members.

Some jurisdictions have suffered from the situation where outside staff, often hired by government, have written a draft committee report and have presented it to the members for approval. This can lead to a loss of independence for the committee and place the government members in a difficult position. Parliaments need to be vigilant in ensuring that the resources provided to the committee are responsible to the committee and not to some outside source such as the government or an interested lobby group. This is necessary to maintain a sense of independence.

There can be great debate as to the correct amount of staff that a committee ideally should have. There is a happy medium between no staff and too many staff which have restricted the members' role as legislators and examiners of the public record. Funds for the research facilities including the library should be allotted by a board or committee made up of representatives of all parties in the House and chaired by the Speaker. If the decisions on how many and what type of services should be provided to members are left in government hands, the result will be predictable. Governments, by their very nature, do not want the Parliament or the committees to be strong. One effective way of limiting the power of Parliament and its members is to starve them of resources under the guise of economy and saving tax money. These same governments do not cut corners in hiring trained staff to advise them and to draft policy. Parliament must take a stand on the amount of services that should be provided to the members to ensure proper review of public legislation and expenditure. Representation of their constituents cannot be provided unless members are given sufficient research tools. Of course, these decisions have to be made in the context of how much a country can afford; but this decision should be left with the Parliament and not with the executive who have a vested interest in starving Parliament.

Rather than having paid researchers working for the committees, it is possible to have volunteer researchers who are interested in the topic under review and happen to have some expertise in the field. Some Parliaments have also accepted the free services of outside advisors who are part of a particular lobby group. The disadvantage of this option is that the lobby group may gain an unfair advantage by having an 'inside track' on advising members about their particular field of interest. If volunteer or 'free' advice is offered, members will have to be vigilant that the advice is independent and still allows the members to make decisions based on all of the available information and differing points of view.

With the computer age, a new tool for research has become available to members and their staff: the internet. With a computer and a connection to the world wide web, researchers, including members, can access data banks around the world. There is no limit to the amount of material that can be found for a relatively small amount of money. A problem can be that there is too much information and that the researcher must find the core of the material that is vital to the project at hand. Telecommunications and the system of electronic messaging have eliminated the miles between countries. Members can enhance their knowledge of a particular matter through a telephone call or an e-mail message to any expert or parliamentarian in another part of the world. Parliaments with inadequate library resources can access other libraries and data banks around the world all through one computer terminal. To use the web effectively takes some training. If Parliaments with good resources, want to help less fortunate Parliaments, courses could be offered either in person or over the net to members and their researchers on how to use the web as an effective research tool. Legislators need not feel isolated as they have the world at their finger tips.

The second most important service to be provided to committees is the facility to enable their meetings to be open to the public. Closed committee meetings may help educate members on the issues before the nation but unless the proceedings are public, the people will not know the issues or the stances taken by the parties and will not be in an informed position come the next election. If pressure groups or interested parties are not allowed to appear before a committee to try to influence public decision making or if members are not allowed to communicate to the public through open committee hearings, the usefulness of the committee comes into question.

The study group debated the merits of having open meetings even when the committee members are debating their final report. By practice, even in Parliaments who have open committee meetings, members have traditionally gone 'in camera' to debate their report. The logic of this procedure was that if the committee was closed, members could be more free to compromise and explore different options than if the public was watching the proceedings. The fear was that if the public could see members exploring different options and points of view in an attempt to find compromise, they would appear to be weak or lacking a strong stance on policy. Some Parliaments are now experimenting with the concept of having all committee meetings open including the report-writing sessions. The proponents of this point of view argue that it is better for the public to see all aspects of parliamentary proceedings and to see members trying to come to a compromise position than to have secret meetings. It may be some time before all committees will feel free to open all their sessions. On the other hand, it has become accepted practice for committees to have open meetings and to make an effort to communicate to the public both through face to face meetings and through the media.

Televising the committee proceedings was the third priority that the study group set for Parliaments. In order for committees to communicate effectively with the public, television broadcasts are one powerful option. The majority of the population will never attend a committee meeting or a sitting of the House. Television may be the only avenue for them to view their members in action and to learn of the issues facing the nation. The television media as well as radio and print do cover highlights of the committee proceedings from time to time but these news items are brief and reflect the bias of the reporter covering the story. If possible, the preferred means of communicating to the public is through 'gavel to gavel' coverage of the proceedings. This eliminates the 'middle man' and ensures that the public has the opportunity to view the entire committee meeting. It may be that only a small proportion of the public will take the time to watch parliamentary proceedings but at least that opportunity is there for them.

In addition to television and other media coverage of the committee proceedings, the study group concluded that the fourth priority for a committee should be travel. If a committee is holding public hearings and seeking the broadest response from the public, it is necessary for the committee to leave the capital city and to go out in the countryside. For countries, such as Canada or Australia, for example, the distances are great and thus the costs can be substantial to have committees travelling to all parts of the nation. Furthermore, extensive travel throughout the country can be time consuming. Other countries may be smaller but suffer from poor roads thus making committee travel difficult. One way that a committee can combat the disadvantages and the costs of travel is to divide the committee into smaller sub-committees and have each travel to a different part of the country. It is important to provide the population with an opportunity to speak with elected members and to have input into public policy. It is true that video conferencing or teleconferencing can be an alternative to committee travel; but it was the belief of the study group that face to face meetings are preferable to telecommunications links. By travelling to other parts of the country, members are also offered a chance to learn about all aspects of that part of the country. This can mean that the member is a better representative of the entire country and not just for their own home community.

A further advantage of having travelling committees is that members of differing parties are given the opportunity to travel and live together for periods of time. They have the opportunity to learn a little about each other and to share differing points of view. In many cases, this has meant that members of opposing parties have a better understanding of the other point of view thus giving more balance to the members of all parties. Travelling committees often become less partisan upon leaving the capital city which can have positive effects for the parliamentary system.

The problem with all of the above priorities or options is that they cost money, money that many governments will argue is not available. This may be true but democracy does have a price and members should be ever vigilant to ensure that the government is not just starving the Parliament to stifle debate or opposition. It is up to the Private Members from both sides of the House to ensure that their committees and Parliament have a fair share of the always limited resources of the country so that there are open and free debates and examinations of the public issues before the nation.

CHAPTER 8

THE ROLE OF PRIVATE MEMBERS

Within any Parliament, either large or small, the Private Member always has to struggle to carve a niche for him/herself in the proceedings. In a large assembly such as the British House of Commons, Private Members have a difficult time being noticed and must expend great energy to be able to express his/her point of view on behalf of their constituents or to make a difference in the public decision making process. Members in one party states find it hard to speak out against the government and thus are limited in their means of contributing to the public good.

A possible solution in any of these circumstances is for the member to serve on a committee and to work hard to make a contribution. Diligent and hard working members can be noticed by the leadership through their work on committees. They can use the committee, especially if it is studying an issue of particular interest or is within the expertise of the member, to promote certain changes or new public policy. Private Members can make a difference through their efforts in committee. Examples of this in Canada are the legislation banning smoking in all federally owned buildings and measures to ensure that all government vehicles would burn fuels other than gasoline as an environmental measure. These were both measures introduced and promoted by Private Members. Even though each measure was a single piece of legislation, considerable effort on the part of the members was needed to pilot the Bills through both Houses, and particularly in committee, to ensure a majority of members voted in favour of the Bills. In both cases, this legislation went against major lobby interests but in the end, the Private Members made a difference and had a direct impact on public legislation. Even if a member does not receive a Cabinet appointment within their term in Parliament, many Private Members have been able to achieve recognition by fighting for particular causes and representing certain interests. Most members who have achieved this goal or recognition were able to do so through their diligent work in committee.

Some members have the feeling that their work is not worthwhile because the government never listens to or acts on the committee's recommendations. Members sometimes have the feeling that committee work is merely a 'make work' project invented by the government to keep members busy and out of mischief. In some cases, this is perhaps true. Members can feel frustrated that their only role seems to be to witness a battle of two teams of experts before the committee and to eventually vote according to the party line as instructed by the whip. Members feel frustrated that they are shifted from one committee to another, filling in for missing members and not becoming expert in the field under consideration. Again, they validly have the impression that they are portable voting machines and not serving a useful purpose within the Parliament. Some members reach a burn-out point and either quit politics or redirect their efforts to answering letters and phone calls from constituents. While this role is important, elected members can be more than 'ombudsmen'. Committees, if effectively organized and with some co-ordination amongst the Private Members from both sides of the House, can be an effective way for Private Members to make a difference. Members have to be prepared to criticize their government from time to time or take an opposing stance from their party in order to represent the wishes of their constituents or their own personal views. If enough Private Members speak out and work together, they can make a difference. They need not be voting machines but can become solid contributors to the parliamentary process. To do this, the Private Members have to convince the government and the whip that they have the best interests of the government and their party at heart. Governments have to be shown that they are not the only ones with all the solutions. Private Members can make a difference in committee.

CHAPTER 9

REPORT STAGE

There are a variety of practices within the Commonwealth as to how committee reports are handled by Parliament and the government. In Jamaica, for example, all committees must report by the end of the year. It is reported that the government does listen to committee advice. On the other hand, governments in Australia do not tend to follow committee recommendations. British governments see the committees as an important way to communicate with the public. In cases where governments do not listen to committee advice, it may be dependent on how insistent and how independently minded the Private Members are. Private Members can press the government to listen and to act.

A committee cannot force a government to take action on a certain issue. Effective committees set realistic goals for themselves and for their governments. To recommend something that is impossible or beyond the financial resources of the country places unrealistic expectations on the government, usually leading to disappointment and failure. Committees can use persuasion and gentle pressure to coax the government to take action. Public hearings with interest groups present, along with public debates in the chamber, help to build pressure on the government to respond to the particular problem. Including the media in the committee meetings and holding briefing sessions with them just before the tabling of a committee report help to ensure that there will be coverage of the committee's findings.

Committee proceedings offer members an opportunity for open debate and independent thinking. With so much of the debate in the House prescribed by decisions taken in caucus and with members often reading speeches in the House, the committee setting offers members the chance to set new directions and to have brief but specific exchanges of ideas and points of view with other committee members and with witnesses.

Two topics that committees often find difficult to explore are estimates and policy for national security and defence spending. Governments are inclined to severely restrict or prevent debate and examination of these topics on the grounds that such debate will infringe on state security. Yet how do members ensure that the money, sometimes substantial, spent for these purposes is in the public interest and is properly accounted for? Some committees have implemented a practice of holding confidential hearings to hear from military or police experts on the condition that the findings will not be made public. Members are able to reassure themselves that the expenditures are valid without revealing state secrets. Similarly, committees reviewing the activities of state-owned corporations often are faced with the assertion from government that certain requested information cannot be released because the corporation would lose a competitive advantage, for example by publicizing the salaries of senior officials or sales figures for the last year. Sometimes, these answers from government are valid; but committees must be ever vigilant that this reason is not being used too often merely as a way of hiding government activities that should be open to the public. Some members might be reluctant to enter closed meetings with an embargo for fear that this will limit their independence and ability to criticize the government. Members have to make a choice as to what price they are willing to pay to see confidential government documents.

One measure of the worth of a committee report is the extent to which it is able to conduct its business in a professional and independent way. If committee reports are written behind the scenes by representatives from the government and presented to the committee for mere ratification by the members, there is little likelihood that the committee report will be taken seriously. This hampers the independence and integrity of the members involved and helps to paint the portrait of members as mere voting machines for the government. Committee reports can have greater credibility if the committee asserts its independence from government in the hearings and in the report writing.

Private Members should have a choice as to which committees they serve on and how long they will stay with that committee. Incidents of the government pulling members off committees without notice greatly limit the independence of the committees and their findings.

To have a truly independent committee chairperson requires that members be free to choose who will occupy the chair. If the chair is independent and seen to be independent, the committee will gain credibility and authority. If the government leader choses the chairperson, the committee will be viewed as a tool of the government.

Lists of potential witnesses and experts should be prepared independently by the committee members and, where possible, government and opposition members should work as colleagues and equals on the committee. If a committee divides habitually along party lines, it will become a mini-chamber and its report will lack the credibility that it could have had. Private Members from both sides of the House must be prepared to work together and independently of government for the sake of the credibility of the committee report.

If government is afraid of public dissent and criticism from an independent committee, then that government is missing an opportunity to use the committee to assess the situation and to recommend solutions. Committees can gain allies by working together with public servants who are usually professional and politically neutral. The public service need not be the enemy and can provide valuable resource material to committee members.

If a committee report is ignored by government, there are several procedures that can be followed. A Parliament can pass a resolution requiring the government to publicly respond either orally or in writing to the committee's recommendations. Public pressure is one way that committees can nudge the government into taking action. If a government does not respond or does so but in a very vague and noncommittal manner, committee members can rely on public pressure to encourage the government to respond further to the committee report.

Members sometimes try to have the Speaker analyse the government's response to see if it is adequate. It is not the role of the Speaker to interpret government responses. This is for the members and ultimately the public to determine whether the government is being secretive or open with plans for change. Governments tend to want to avoid charges of being closed or secretive and will often respond by openly complying with a committee's recommendation.

A problem for a committee, and for the government, is whether once the public will has been assessed as accurately as possible, the government should lead the country toward a higher goal or merely follow. Successful governments usually combine leadership with a keen sense of wanting to be in touch with the public mood. Decisions to make changes for the best interests of the country might be opposite to the public mood but governments usually try to make these decisions early enough in their mandate to allow for the measures to show positive results before the next election. Governments who have just come through a period of restraint and cutbacks in order to eliminate budget deficits know that they have to show the people the positive results of balanced books before the next election. Committee reports can help governments by assessing the public mood and acting as a sounding board for government proposed policies. In the ideal, governments would rely on independent advice from Parliamentary Committees and would combine leadership with popular support to design policies that will benefit the country.

Unfortunately, the ideal is hard to achieve in politics and governments are not always open to advice from committees, even if it is based on sound analysis and direct input from the people. Committee members have to know when to assert their independence without losing their places within their political parties and power structures. This is a difficult balancing act that members constantly have to attempt.

CHAPTER 10

THE FUTURE OF THE COMMITTEE SYSTEM

Committees have changed over the years and are ever adapting to the new expectations placed on them and on Parliament. To remain relevant, committees will have to continue to change and evolve. The main purpose of a committee, and in fact, of the Parliament is to hold the government accountable. As government continues to play an important role in the development of society and the provision of public services such as health care and education, Parliament through its committees will have to bolster its efforts to review government policy and expenditure estimates and report to the people.

Members of the study group compiled a list of possible ways that committees could strengthen themselves and improve the overall operation of Parliament. These points are not recommendations but 'positive options'. Each Parliament cannot take this complete list and adopt it as the recipe for a model Parliament. The circumstances, the needs and problems in each Parliament are very different. What will work in one political culture will not necessarily work in another. It should also be noted that the following positive options were not all agreed upon unanimously but are the reflection of a variety of points of view. The study group is of the hope that Parliaments throughout the Commonwealth will find some of the options useful to them in their situation as they review procedures and consider ways of strengthening their committee structures.

The study group offers 21 positive options for consideration:

(1) Membership on the committees should be based on the member's experience and professional training. Members of Parliament with specific expertise should be invited to apply this experience to the tasks facing a committee. Members of the study group were aware of the counter argument that members could be viewed as having vested professional interests and thus should not be on committees specializing in that particular field. On balance, the group believed that the issues of the world are becoming so specialized that members trained in specific fields could be helpful to the committee without necessarily having a conflict of interest.

(2) In order to build a greater degree of experience on a committee, all committees should be established for the life of the Parliament (likely four years on average). When members have longer to work together and to share their collective expertise, the committee will be considerably stronger.

(3) In the same light, substitutions of members on committees should be reduced and made more difficult to achieve. New members put on a committee at a moment's notice and without the background of the subject under investigation will be there only as a replacement and following orders from the whip. This is hardly a way to build either expertise or independence on the committee.

(4) Have committees smaller, thus making it easier for members to plan committee hearings when everyone can attend and thus avoiding the necessity for substitutions.

(5) The size of the committees should be a reflection of the size and resources of the particular House. No one formula can be outlined as to the ideal size of a committee.

(6) The study group clearly saw the need for more independently minded members who would be willing to work together for the betterment of the Parliament and would resist the undue influence of the party whip.

(7) The success of any committee will be determined by the amount of research resources that are made available to the committee. Members cannot be expected to be knowledgeable about every topic. Committee members are expected to be prepared on many topics within a short period of time and be able to match wits with experienced public servants. No member has the time to do all of this and keep in touch with their constituents. Research resources in the form of either personal or caucus researchers, resources through a parliamentary library and access to the world wide web should and could be provided to members. Decisions on the provisions of these services ideally should be made by Parliament itself through a board or committee on parliamentary administration. This means that members would decide on services to members. With the information explosion, members need assistance in collecting, sorting and assessing this information and applying it to the proceedings in the House and committee.

(8) Committees should be organized along the lines of government itself. Committees should be established to match key governmental departments. More emphasis could be placed on the review of estimates to ensure prudent spending by government. In order to motivate members to devote time to the review of estimates, members could be empowered to shift the priorities of the estimates by raising some votes and lowering others as long as the totals were not increased. Cabinet's responsibility for the collection of taxes and control of the public purse must be respected but members have to be given some incentive to review estimates other than to just watch for government mismanagement.

(9) All-party committees could be utilized in place of public commissions and would likely report in a shorter period of time at less cost.

Commissions and judicial inquiries tend to be batteries of lawyers battling it out to protect their own group of interests. Parliamentary committees, especially if they were politically neutral, could provide political insight into the problem and could offer recommendations that might be more acceptable to government. Committee reports would perhaps not sit on book shelves quite as much as commission reports and would cost considerably less.

(10) For bicameral Houses, prestudy is an option. Usually, government Bills are introduced by a minister in the lower House. In order to save some time and to review the Bill more thoroughly, the upper House could also review the clauses of the Bill before it passes the lower House. Amendments suggested by the upper House could then be incorporated by the lower House in its committee review. Once the lower House has finished its review, the upper House could pass the Bill expeditiously knowing that its amendments have already been incorporated into the Bill.

There are two disadvantages to prestudy for the upper House. With prestudy, the amendments sent by the upper House to the lower House are often credited to the lower House while the upper House gets none of the credit for the improvements to the Bill. Critics of upper Chambers also claim that legislation passes through the upper House without a word and that this demonstrates there is no point in having an upper House. This argument fails to acknowledge that the upper House has been working on the Bill for some time before its formal review of the Bill. In both cases, the upper House is usually not given credit for the hard work it has done. However, prestudy does improve the efficiency of the handling of the legislation through Parliament.

(11) Some Houses have experimented with reference of a Bill to committee before second reading. A Bill that has not yet been approved in principle is much more open to amendment than after second reading. Once the Bill has passed committee, it would be sent to third reading and approval. The criticism of this option is that there would be little or no debate in the Chamber on the Bill thus reducing the chance for the opposition to publicly debate the Bill. Approval in principle could still be done in the Chamber after committee review but this would take as much time as the present procedure. At least there would be more opportunity for amendment before approval in principle.

(12) Some Houses have experimented with the drafting of Bills in principle before the government introduces them into the chamber. This option gives Private Members a greater opportunity to design and draft legislation before it is introduced and the sides are drawn in the debate. But opposition members may ask why they should work hard to improve legislation, consequently, making the government look better. This option

does offer a more constructive role for Private Members, but it does co-opt opposition members and could prevent them from speaking critically of the Bill during consideration by the Parliament. There are advantages and disadvantages to this option.

(13) Steps should be taken to enhance the role of the Private Member in Parliament and reduce the partisan party control over members. In many Houses, Private Members are reduced to being voting machines. Reinvigorated committees with more independent members would revitalize the Parliament and give members a useful role to fill. This in turn could improve Parliament's public image. Members being able to truly represent their constituents rather than being pawns in the hands of the party whips would improve the public perception of politics and elected members.

(14) Some countries, such as New Zealand, have implemented a form of proportional representation in order to make Parliament more representative of the various shades of opinion which constitute the public will. Although there was no consensus on this point in the study group, it was conceded that a government which has a small majority or which relies on a coalition of parties to remain in power is more responsive to members and their views. The New Zealand model of MMP by its very nature virtually ensures that government will not likely achieve a majority in Parliament and this, it is argued, enhances the role of Private Members.

(15) As a positive option, international treaties should be examined and ratified by Parliament before being signed by the Prime Minister. Frequently, the Parliament is in the situation of having to pass an Act to ratify a treaty well after it has been signed thus leaving the Parliament facing a 'fait accompli'.

(16) It was strongly agreed that Parliaments should be spending more time in committee reviewing proposed estimates and holding ministers to account for where the money has been spent and where it will be dedicated for the coming year. In order to make the estimate review worthwhile, it was suggested that members be given the power to move motions to reduce certain items and increase others as long as the overall budgetary amounts were not changed. Respect for the principle of the government's control over the raising of taxes and expenditure have to be maintained within the Westminster model, but Private Members could have some leeway without infringing on the government prerogative. Giving Private Members some scope for change and not just review would make the estimate process much more attractive to members and would enhance their role in the parliamentary process.

(17) Wider powers of inquiry should be given to committees without having to go back to the House for approval. True investigation by Private

Members without the permission of the executive could enhance the role of Parliament and, particularly, the Private Member.

(18) Chairs of the various committees should be divided up amongst the various parties represented in the House. If committees are to be more non-partisan and an area where Private Members can contribute to the parliamentary process, less control by government of the committee chairs would be advantageous.

(19) Parliament should set its own budget as well as that for committees. Governments, if given the option of granting money for the operation of Parliament will chose to starve it in the hopes of weakening the source of criticism and delay. In the long run, healthy committees can create stronger and more accountable governments but it is rare for a government to see this long term advantage.

(20) Modern technological inventions such as teleconferencing, video conferencing, electronic mail and the world wide web are all tools that a modern Parliament can use to its advantage. Where possible, these new technological inventions should be used to improve Parliament's research methods and communication between Parliaments and between the members and their constituents.

(21) In order to strengthen Parliament and its committees, a less partisan approach should be used in the formation of the committees and in their proceedings. If Private Members continue to be ignored by the executive or are thought of as foot soldiers there only to protect the government and the party regardless of the issue, the existing cynicism amongst the public and the sense of discouragement amongst the members will only increase. A more relaxed party stance in committee and the enhancement of the role of Private Members will do much to improve the way people accept Parliament and politics.

If even a few of the above positive options are adopted by a Parliament, a marked improvement in the performance of that House and its committees will be noticed. No government will willingly reduce its own powers. It is up to the Private Members to assert themselves as useful members of the Parliament and to assume an important role in the review of legislation, estimates and in holding government accountable.

KC Wheare has observed that there are six basic roles of Parliamentary Committees: '... to advise; to inquire; to administer; to legislate; to negotiate; and to scrutinize and control'.[1] These six basic roles can only be fulfilled if Private Members take some initiative in asserting their independence.

1 Wheare, KC, *Government by Committee: An Essay on the British Constitution*, 1965, Oxford: Clarendon.

In the ideal, more independent members working in effective committees will provide a better review of government activities, greater government accountability and a more thorough surveillance of the ever increasing role government plays in society. In the Westminster model, committees will never play the role that the American congressional committees do. The American committees, and in fact Congress, can exercise greater independence because they are subject to presidential veto. The American system is one of checks and balances that often give the appearance of stalemate.

The congressional model, as practised in the United States, has a further drawback in that the committee review of Presidential appointments causes some good candidates either to decline the nomination to avoid the intrusive investigation or to be dropped due to political deal making.

On the other hand, the Westminster model provides for the check and balance within the Parliament. Governments, to survive, must maintain a majority within the House and for this reason usually have stronger party discipline in order to keep members in line. The government, with a majority, is assured of getting its legislative and budgetary program through Parliament at the expense of limiting the powers of the Private Members and the committees. The study group has concluded that even though parliamentary-style committees will never be as powerful as those seen in the American congressional system, improvements could be made within Parliamentary Committees if the Private Members are given more independence to investigate and question.

If the committees were to be given more power, would this be at the expense of the power of the executive? Not necessarily. Power is not necessarily finite. Committees, and, thus, Private Members could be given a larger role in the parliamentary process with the result that the executive would have better advice and clearer communication with the people, thus enhancing its own power.

The study group concluded that the future is bright for the Parliamentary Committees and has offered 21 positive options for consideration. Committees will continue to evolve and adapt to the changing needs of the people. The common theme throughout the positive options is that the role of the Private Member must be enhanced and this can be done through the committees. This will be a complementary relationship. As the committees are strengthened, so too will the role of the Private Member. As Private Members assume new roles and responsibilities, they will enhance the role of the committees and ultimately restore some of the public confidence in Parliament and politics. It is up to Private Members throughout the Commonwealth to seize the moment and to use their talents to strengthen their roles within the parliamentary system as the Westminster model of democratic governance moves into the new millennium.

CHAPTER 11

OCCUPANTS OF THE CHAIR

Jim Anderton, MP, New Zealand

INTRODUCTION

With the advent of the election of the first MMP (Mixed-Member Proportional) Parliament in New Zealand in 1996, there have been a number of interesting developments that have affected the position of chairperson of a Select Committee. These are discussed below from a New Zealand perspective with some comparisons with the United Kingdom and the Australian House of Representatives if they are known to have different practices. However, I am no expert on the systems in these countries and I assume that other members of the study group will be able to supply more comprehensive comparisons when we meet formally.

The change of electoral system came about through increasing concern that Parliament was not seen as very representative and that there was too much power in the hands of the executive in relation to the legislature, which was able to be dominated by one political party. In 1986, a Commission of Inquiry recommended the adoption of an MMP system based on the system operating in Germany. While there was not a lot of enthusiasm for the proposed change among the two main political parties, public opinion kept the issue alive and it was eventually the subject of two referendums. In 1993 the electorate voted to adopt the new system and the 1996 general election was the first held under the new system.

By way of clarification, all of the House's committees in New Zealand (apart from the Committee of the Whole House) are known as 'Select Committees' and are referred to as such in this paper. I am aware that some other systems distinguish between 'Select Committees' and 'Standing Committees' but we make no such distinction in New Zealand.

METHOD OF SELECTION OF THE CHAIRPERSON

Apart from two specialist committees, all the Select Committees in New Zealand elect their own chairperson. The exceptions are the Officers of Parliament Committee and the Business Committee, for which Standing

Orders provide that the Speaker be the chairperson. Until 1996, the chairperson was elected for the life of the Parliament but this has now changed and a member can give seven days' notice of his/her intention to move in the committee that a chairperson be removed from office. Removal from office has not occurred since this provision came into operation.

While the formality of the election takes place at the first committee meeting (the election being presided over by the clerk of the committee), the political reality is that a lot of negotiation goes on behind the scenes and the news media generally carry fairly accurate reports on who will chair particular committees before they have actually been elected. The behind the scenes process is discussed more fully on p 46, in the section headed 'Are all Chairpersons from the Government?'.

In the United Kingdom House of Commons, it appears that the Speaker appoints the chairperson of a Standing Committee while a Select Committee generally elects its chairperson.[1] In the Australian House of Representatives each committee elects its chairperson.[2]

ROLE OF THE CHAIRPERSON

This section is largely drawn from a publication prepared by the Office of the Clerk of the House of Representatives entitled *Effective Select Committee Membership*.[3]

Functions

The chairperson of a Select Committee is responsible for chairing committee meetings and ruling on procedural and relevance issues. Such matters might involve the relevance of questions or amendments. He/she might also range to dealing with disorder among members or by the public, and where members will sit during meetings if this is a subject of dispute.

On occasions, the chairperson will be required to answer oral questions in the House on committee business. These are on notice in the same form as those asked of ministers and come at the end of questions to ministers. They do not occur frequently and often relate to a particular item of business of interest to the member asking the question.

1 Erskine May, T, *Treatise on The Law, Privileges, Proceedings and Usage of Parliament*, 2nd edn, 1989, London, pp 590, 620.

2 Barlin, LM (ed), *House of Representatives Practice*, 3rd edn, 1997, Canberra, p 593.

3 *Effective Select Committee Membership: A Guide for Chairpersons and Members of Parliament*, Office of the Clerk of the House of Representatives, 1997, Wellington.

Powers

There are some executive powers conferred on chairpersons by Standing Orders and there are only a small number of occasions when the chairperson has the authority to act on behalf of the committee. The chairperson does the following:

- sets a meeting (in Wellington only) and agenda in the absence of a committee decision;
- makes a public statement on the nature of the committee's consideration of a matter, subject to the committee's consent;
- signs a committee report;
- speaks first in the House when a report is debated;
- speaks first in the House during the relevant part of Estimates or financial review debates;
- requests, on behalf of the committee, the appearance of witnesses or the production of papers;
- signs a summons for a person to attend or to produce papers or records, subject to committee direction;
- orders the withdrawal of disorderly visitors, including members of Parliament who are not members of the committee;
- decides if a committee member should be disqualified from participation in proceedings due to apparent bias;
- rules on the relevance of questions to witnesses.

Meeting management

The chairperson needs to ensure that the agenda meets the committee's needs and that the programme of business is kept up to date. Particular leadership skills may need to be exercised when a committee is trying to work through a large amount of business. If additional time is given to one item of business, it may affect how much can be spent on another. The chairperson maintains a constant overview of this and reminds members whenever the programme might need adjustment to ensure reporting deadlines are met.

The chairperson can cancel a meeting he/she has set but not one that the committee has set. Cancellation of a meeting set by the committee needs to be with the agreement of all of the committee's members.

Conduct of hearings

The chairperson is in control of hearing of evidence and directs the proceedings. However, this is subject to the approval of the committee. To ensure the hearings run smoothly, a chairperson normally discusses how he/she proposes conducting the hearing before the meeting is opened to the public.

The chairperson has a significant responsibility to ensure that the principles of natural justice are followed when witnesses are being heard, as provided in Standing Orders. In particular, provisions include the right of a person to respond to allegations that may seriously damage his/her reputation, the right for a witness to ask to be heard in private or secret and the right to object to answering a question.

Behind the scenes

An effective chairperson will also be working behind the scenes with the government and other members of the Select Committee on the progress of important legislation and will maintain open communication channels with all committee members. This ensures the smooth running of the committee's program, in which the chairperson should be taking an active interest.

ARE ALL CHAIRPERSONS FROM THE GOVERNMENT?

While the Standing Orders do not specify that chairpersons represent the government, the reality is that they generally do. Prior to the MMP electoral system, the electoral system generally returned successive governments that were able to manage Parliament to the extent that it was seen by many as a rubber stamp for the executive. Therefore, Select Committees appointed by the House had a government majority and the government nominee was able to obtain the necessary votes to be elected as chairperson. He/she usually stayed in office for the life of the Parliament and this ensured ongoing control. Therefore, the constitutional principle of Parliament being sovereign, with the executive being subordinate and accountable to it was somewhat blurred by successive governments' controlling mechanisms. The Regulations Review Committee became an exception to executive domination of Select Committees and this committee has traditionally been chaired by an opposition member even though the government maintained a majority on the committee itself.

Since the election of the first MMP Parliament and the introduction of new Standing Orders, the outcome of elections for the position of chairperson is less certain. Our Standing Orders require membership of Select Committees to be in proportion to party representation in the House. We now have a coalition government that has 61 of the 120 seats in the House. With this proportion applied to each of the Select Committees (generally eight or 10 members), the government is not entitled to have a majority on any committee. To avoid the prospect of tied votes on the elections for chairpersons, the government came to an arrangement with another party (ACT – generally considered to be on the government's side of the political spectrum) whereby that party's members on Select Committees would support the government's candidates in exchange for government members supporting that party's candidate for one committee. The main opposition parties were, therefore, shut out of any opportunity to chair any committees apart from the Regulations Review Committee as discussed above and two committees where ACT had no representation. Perhaps surprisingly, in the case of the latter two the government nominees were successfully elected even though a tie might have been expected. This was because the party I lead (Alliance) decided to co-operate for a number of reasons, including getting both of our Maori members of Parliament on the Maori Affairs Committee and the need to avoid deadlock.

The end result has been the 'winner takes all' approach that was a feature of the first-past-the-post system. However, my opinion is that a proportional system would be better reflected by a broad agreement for chairpersons to be drawn from parties in proportion to their representation in the House. This would contribute further to the key role Select Committees can play in reasserting control over the executive, which was one of the key factors behind the change in the electoral system.

Regardless of the end result, the fact remains that while the committees go through the formalities of electing chairpersons, the real decisions have generally already been made outside the committee. As we will see below, nominees can often be those who, for various reasons, miss out on other appointments such as Cabinet positions. The government is the predominant factor in such decisions and the ability to negotiate a trade-off currently depends on how much co-operation is needed to get as many government chairpersons as possible.

IS THE CHAIRPERSON IN TRAINING FOR CABINET OR THE SPEAKERSHIP?

In New Zealand under the previous electoral system, a committee chairperson was traditionally a member on the 'ascendant' who, if he/she progressed government business with due diligence and in line with government policy, could expect at some time in the future to be considered for a position particularly as a minister but possibly as a presiding officer. The chances of a competent chairperson obtaining higher executive office were reasonably high if his/her party was elected to govern and if he/she retained a seat in the House. This is based on simple arithmetic. With a total of less than 100 members of Parliament, there were still 20 Cabinet ministers and often a number (six would be common) of ministers or Under Secretaries outside Cabinet. Those positions were filled by members with previous executive experience and those who had performed well as committee chairpersons or backbenchers in the past. Depending on the number of retirements there had been and the size of the swing to or from the governing party, there may not be an extensive range of experience to choose from in forming the Cabinet once the new members and those who have not performed well in the past are eliminated. Therefore, an ambitious and competent politician could definitely expect to progress through chairing a committee to Cabinet.

The interesting question that this career path raises is whether being a parliamentarian is a career in itself. As the proportion of members of Parliament to ministers increases, I think more members are likely to see this as a career option and that chairing a committee could be a realistic ambition in itself as the chances of reaching Cabinet diminish. This would be a beneficial development because the interests of Parliament are likely to come before the government's and it encourages independence from the government to some extent. More attention might be given to due process and a chairperson's reputation judged on management of the committee's business in a fair and inclusive manner. Now that we have 120 members of Parliament with the introduction of MMP, I believe we have a more parliamentary focus on Select Committee business and that this will produce better long term results.

Our first MMP election has resulted in a coalition government, the senior partner of which formed the previous government on its own. To make way in Cabinet for ministers from the junior coalition partner, there was no longer a place in Cabinet or as ministers outside Cabinet for some former Cabinet ministers or ministers outside Cabinet. Some of them are now chairpersons of Select Committees and in their cases, the career path has been turned around somewhat. Some of these members might have some cause for disaffection, which might be expected to contribute to taking a more independent line as a chairperson.

As far as being a chairperson forming part of a career path to becoming the Speaker is concerned, I am not aware of any of our recent Speakers having progressed in that manner. A more common scenario is the need to provide ministerial openings for high-performing backbenchers and the movement of a senior minister to the Speakership can and has facilitated this in the past.

MUST AN EFFECTIVE CHAIRPERSON BE NEUTRAL OR IS HE/SHE THE LEADER OF THE INQUIRY?

First, this question presupposes that committees conduct inquiries only. This is not the case in New Zealand, where almost every Bill is also considered by a

Select Committee, which often results in considerable redrafting. Our committees also regularly examine performance of public sector organisations, public sector spending plans (Estimates) and petitions.

I think it is important to consider the difference between the terms 'neutral' and 'fair'. Our committees are fairly small compared with those in the United Kingdom and Australia and I cannot see any merit in expecting the chairperson to remain neutral. To do so would be to take the politics out of politics and those who seek neutrality should consider the options provided by the courts and commissions of inquiry. However, a chairperson does have a responsibility to ensure a fair and reasonable process is followed and that all interests are taken into account.

The question of leadership can depend on the dynamics of a particular committee and the nature of an item of business. Naturally, a good chairperson will exercise leadership by managing committee business effectively and by speaking for the committee when necessary. However, in the absence of such leadership, an effective opposition member can sometimes exercise considerable influence.

An important consideration in New Zealand is that with our current proportions on committees and the increasing independence of some government members, a committee could initiate (by majority vote) an inquiry[4] that is not supported by the chairperson. Under these circumstances, the chairperson would be expected to be fair and ensure that the majority decision is respected. A chairperson in this position would then be expected to take responsibility for progressing the inquiry even though he/she might ultimately be part of a minority view expressed in the final report.

OTHER ISSUES

In addition to the issues listed for discussion, further issues of possible interest are set out below.

Casting vote

Our recent developments in adapting Standing Orders to meet the needs of MMP resulted in a change to the use of a casting vote. Prior to 1996, the chairperson of a Select Committee had a deliberative vote and, if the votes were tied, a casting vote. There was no convention about how the casting vote would be used, unlike the House where the casting vote of the Speaker was

4 Unlike many other systems, our committees can initiate their own inquiries and do not need a referral from the House.

expected to be exercised in favour of the *status quo*. Therefore, the chairperson's casting vote was exercised in the same direction as the deliberative vote and could be used in favour of change rather than the *status quo*. The chairperson no longer has a casting vote and a tied vote is now declared lost. The same applies in the House and it was done to ensure proportionality is maintained. This change resulted in an impasse on one committee recently and the situation was resolved by the committee reporting a bill back to the House and informing the House that a tied vote had meant the committee could not reach a decision. This left the House to decide if the bill would proceed and it was defeated at that stage.

I note that in the Australian House of Representatives and the British House of Commons the chairperson has only a casting vote and no deliberative vote.[5]

Deputy chairperson

Until 1997, our Select Committees did not have deputy chairpersons. We have yet to establish a distinct role for this person and he/she can assume the powers of the chairperson only in the event of absence from New Zealand or absence during a meeting. In other words, if the chairperson is not in Wellington for a meeting, the deputy chairperson can take over during the meeting but any executive powers immediately revert to the chairperson after the meeting provided he/she remains in New Zealand. This could raise particular problems if the chairperson is sick. Most of the deputy chairpersons elected by our current Select Committees are from parties in the coalition government but there are some from opposition parties.

It appears that there is no formal provision for deputy chairpersons in the United Kingdom but that the Australian House of Representatives generally provides for the election of a deputy chairperson and that this person is normally an opposition member.[6] I am particularly interested in following up how this role has developed in other Parliaments and how it has worked having an opposition member taking over in the chairperson's absence.

Payment to committee chairpersons

Until 1996, chairpersons of Select Committees were not paid any more than a backbench member of Parliament. This had been a matter of some concern to many members and provided little incentive to take on the additional

5 *Op cit*, Barlin, fn 2, p 595; *op cit*, Erskine May, fn 1, pp 606, 623.

6 *Op cit*, Barlin, fn 2, p 596.

responsibilities and pursue a parliamentary career path. Since the 1996 election, chairpersons are now paid an additional NZ$3,000 on top of their standard salaries. This figure was determined by the Higher Salaries Commission, which is an independent body that sets the salaries of members of Parliament, senior public servants, etc.

CONCLUSION

I have shown in this chapter that changes in our electoral system have contributed, to a small extent, to a power shift away from the government of the day to Parliament and, in particular, Select Committees. Parliamentary developments are less predictable and based more on cooperation, although the coalition government is still doing as much as it can to minimise the effects of this power shift by continuing to seek control of Select Committees by ensuring their own nominees are elected to the key roles of chairing committees. As we become more comfortable with our new system of proportional representation, there is potential for this development to consolidate and extend.

The chairperson of a Select Committee has a very significant responsibility to facilitate committee business and to maintain effective communication between parties. As the MMP system takes root, chairpersons who follow the old pattern of 'taking instructions' from the minister will find it harder to function, while those who demonstrate some independent thought and adhere to fair management practices will build solid reputations as parliamentarians.

CHAPTER 12

THE FUTURE OF THE COMMITTEE SYSTEM

Jim Anderton, MP, New Zealand

INTRODUCTION

The election of the 45th Parliament in New Zealand, the first to be elected under the MMP (Mixed-Member Proportional) system, has been accompanied by a number of changes to the committee system. This chapter focuses on the future of the New Zealand committee system and provides information and opinion as a basis for comparison with other systems.

It is important to note that all New Zealand Parliamentary Committees are called 'Select Committees'. We do not make the distinctions between committees based on their purpose or the business before them as do some other Commonwealth systems.

There are 18 Select Committees in New Zealand at present; 12 subject committees and six special purpose committees.

NECESSITY OF THE COMMITTEE SYSTEM

In New Zealand, Select Committees (as a branch of the legislature) are separate and distinct from the government (the executive). Select committees do not play a role in facilitating communication between the government and the public. All committee business is originated in and referred by the House of Representatives and committees report their findings to the House.

While committees do not play a direct role in communication between the government and the public, they do play an important role in enabling the public to comment on government policy. Indeed, New Zealand can justifiably claim to be a world leader in the extent to which the public may have input into the democratic process.

The public is able to make written and oral submissions on almost all legislation before the House of Representatives. The exceptions to this rule are legislation passed under urgency (such as the recent controversial State Services Amendment Bill) and certain financial Bills (Appropriation and Imtrest Supply Bills). Generally, committees operate on the basis that Bills are referred to them for scrutiny and criticism and public evidence forms the bulk of this criticism.[1] They advertise for submissions in major daily newspapers and now frequently travel throughout New Zealand hearing evidence. Submissions are received on virtually every Bill though the number may range from a very few to several thousand, depending on the content of the Bill and the level of public interest in the policy it seeks to enact.

The other common way that the public may comment on the actions or policies of the government is by petitioning the House of Representatives. Petitions are presented by a member of Parliament and usually relate to matters of public policy such as the state of the public health system or matters affecting the conservation of forests. However, petitions may also relate to personal grievances such as unfair dismissal. A petition relating to a personal grievance can only be presented once all other avenues of legal redress have been exhausted. A petition is allocated to an appropriate Select Committee for consideration and report to the House. The committee usually invites submissions from those directly concerned with the petition. In exceptional circumstances, a committee may advertise for submissions from the general public on a petition. Most recently, the Government Administration Committee called for public submissions on a petition seeking to prevent the construction of a new ministerial building.

EVOLUTION OF THE COMMITTEE STRUCTURE

The present Select Committee structure was adopted in 1985 with the aim of strengthening the accountability of the government to Parliament. However, the role of Select Committees had been growing and changing since the 1960s when they began to scrutinise some government legislation. This growth is reflected in changes to Standing Orders in 1979. However, at that time, committees did little work apart from scrutinising legislation.[2] The 1985 reforms established a new structure for Select Committees to place every major aspect of government policy, administration, and finance within the jurisdiction of a Select Committee. This structure which remains today, with some modification, has enabled Select Committees to become the 'workhorses' of the New Zealand Parliament.

Since 1985, the most substantial changes to the committee structure occurred in 1996, in preparation for the first MMP Parliament. Some of the important changes included:

1 McGee, DG, *Parliamentary Practice in New Zealand*, 1994, Wellington, p 230.

2 Palmer, G, *New Zealand's Constitution in Crisis*, 1992, Dunedin, pp 110–13.

- the development of the practice of committees inviting Ministers responsible for specific Bills to brief them and to appear before committees to be questioned during the examination of estimates;
- a requirement that Bills be reported to the House within six months of being referred to a committee. This ensures the ongoing progress of all Bills, even those without government support;
- the ability of committees to divide Bills to enable them to retain contentious or complex portions of Bills for further consideration while reporting the rest of the Bill to the House;
- the broadening of committee portfolios which used to relate only to the scrutiny of the public sector. Portfolios now encompass subject areas which allows significantly wider use of a committee's inquiry powers; and
- the application of natural justice provisions to committee proceeding such as the right to have evidence heard in private or secret, the right to be accompanied by counsel, the right to make a submission on proposed committee findings which may damage one's reputation, a person's right to respond to allegations made against them and the right to object to answering a question. The aim is to ensure that the committee process is fair and unbiased.[3]

The New Zealand committee system has undergone considerable change to reach its present form and there is no reason to think that there will not be further changes. Evolution of the committee system is likely once Parliament gains greater experience of operating in the MMP environment. It is likely that some systems introduced in anticipation of MMP will require amendment and that new procedures will have to be devised to deal with unanticipated eventualities. Indeed, some alterations were made in 1996 following a review of the operation of Standing Orders.[4]

Already, the House's sitting hours are clashing with the meetings of Select Committee due to the fact that committees do not all meet simultaneously as was anticipated. The sitting hours of the House are currently under review.

Another interesting development has been the proposal, by the Clerk of the House of Representatives, that the House take a greater role in approving treaties and other international agreements before the government ratifies them. At present the government, without any need for approval from or consultation with the House, may enter into treaties. The implementation of some treaties requires the House to pass legislation yet the House plays no part in considering the treaty that obliges it to legislate. A recent example of

3 Report of the Standing Orders Committee on the Review of Standing Orders, 1.18A, 1995.

4 Report of the Standing Orders Committee on its Review of the Operation of Standing Orders, 1.18B, 1996.

this occurrence was the Chemical Weapons (Prohibition) Act 1996 which implemented the 'Convention on the Prohibition of the Development, Production, Stockpiling and Use of Chemical Weapons and on their Destruction'. Other substantial future examples might include the Multilateral Agreement on Investment.

The Clerk of the House proposes that all draft treaties be approved by the House prior to ratification and recommends that draft treaties be referred to the appropriate subject Select Committee for consideration. The implementation of these proposals would create a new role for Select Committees, particularly for the Foreign Affairs, Defence and Trade Committee which would play a central co-ordinating role in allocating draft treaties to the appropriate Select Committee. The proposal has not yet been discussed in any detail by the House and may prove to be politically controversial.

EFFECTIVENESS OF THE COMMITTEE SYSTEM

Select Committees achieve the goals of scrutiny of the executive and the facilitating of public input into the legislative process. The committees are considering an ever-increasing amount of legislation and are conducting thorough and useful inquiries. However, while they are conducting a great deal of productive bipartisan work, some deficiencies can be identified.

The legislative work of Parliament is so great that legislation dominates the time of many committees. Time must also be found to examine estimates and review the performance of government departments, Crown entities and public organisations on an annual basis. The consideration of Bills, estimates and financial reviews is carried out under tight time constraints with the result that not all items of business receive the attention they deserve. Members devote large amounts of their time and effort to Select Committees but conflicting demands on their time and the limited time available to conduct committee business impact on the committees' effectiveness.

Another problem that has not been alleviated as a result of MMP is that of numbers. In previous parliaments, the 99 members were stretched thinly across 18 committees. This was exacerbated by Cabinet Ministers not being members of committees. Most members were members of two committees while at least one member served on four. The difficulties this caused for the smaller parties in Parliament were considerable. It was expected that this problem would be addressed by the increase to 120 members in the MMP parliament, where, even after a 20 member Cabinet was excluded, members would serve on one subject committee only.[5]

5 Report of the Standing Orders Committee on the Review of Standing Orders, 1.18A, 1995.

However, the small size of the coalition government majority and a desire to minimise the power of Parliament over the executive has had a serious impact on the operation of Select Committees. The government acted to ensure it held half the positions on each Select Committee, resulting in half of the committees meeting on Wednesdays and half meeting on Thursdays. This enabled government members to attend more than one committee each week and to avoid being in a minority, despite their small majority in the House. Most committees are chaired by government members, have government deputy chairpersons and are dominated by government members in combination with members who vote with the government. Some committees are evenly divided between government and opposition members. This can act to stifle government action but does nothing to empower the opposition to act contrary to government wishes.[6] This is not to say that committees cannot act independently of the government (a number have done so) [7] but this can occur only with the support of government members.

The results of the government acting to avoid being in a minority on committees and of an increase in the size of many committees are that most members of Parliament are, again, members of more than one committee. This is an inefficient use of resources which leads to clashes between the sittings of the House and meetings of committees. Membership of more than one committee also prevents members from developing expertise in a particular portfolio area as they must divide their time and attention between two or more committees.

A system where members are thinly spread across committees does not have a great deal of flexibility. As a result, members are required to substitute for permanent committee members. Substitute members are not always interested in the work of the committee and seldom have time to adequately prepare. Substitution of an experienced or interested member on to a committee for consideration of a specific issue can be valuable, but the practice of wholesale substitution has little to recommend it.

The deficiencies outlined above could be remedied by reducing the membership of committees to eight members each and by the government relaxing its control over committees. This latter step seems unlikely to occur at present. It should also be remembered that, while committees do valuable work, they have recommendatory powers only. What is required is an acceptance by government that the role of committees is to scrutinise the performance of the government and this should continue regardless of the political affiliations of those who chair committees, and that there is no danger

6 A drawn vote is resolved in the negative in the New Zealand House of Representatives.

7 The Government Administration Committee is evenly divided between government and non-government members. Recently, the committee was highly critical of government plans to build a ministerial building.

in allowing a more efficient and representative committee system to operate, especially in an MMP environment where this is an expectation of voters.

MMP was designed to produce a more representative parliament and to assert the primacy of Parliament over the executive. Under MMP, it is most unlikely that any one political party will be able to form the executive. It is also unlikely that the executive will hold such a large majority that it can absolutely control Parliament. If MMP is to work properly, I believe the chairing of Select Committees should be shared by all parties in Parliament and committees should not all automatically contain government majorities. In addition, committees should receive their own appropriations from which to conduct their business and to employ specialist advisers. I understand that committees in some other countries do hold their own budgets and I would be interested in hearing more about how they operate.

CONCLUSION

The role of committees is likely to continue to develop in New Zealand. It is also likely that inquiries conducted by committees will grow in number and scope as members come to terms with the wide-ranging nature of the inquiry powers. Comparison of Commonwealth committee systems with the United States Congressional committee system is particularly interesting, given the similarities of colonial background and the fact that all systems are modelled on the Westminster system to some extent.

Some features of the United States Congressional committee system already exist in the New Zealand Select Committee structure. The powers of the Rules Committee to set limits on debates and control the flow of business in the United States House of Representatives are similar to those of the recently established Business Committee in New Zealand. Both play a role in regulating the business of the House, though the Rules Committee's powers go further, allowing it to regulate how Bills may be amended and to initiate legislation.[8]

The power of Congress legislative committees to initiate legislation is also far removed from New Zealand's current system where committees scrutinise legislation after it is drafted and introduced to the House. While individual members may promote Bills, committees do not have a similar ability in New Zealand. In recent years, very few members' Bills have passed into law and this suggests unwillingness on the part of the government to loosen its control of the legislative process. The tradition of assertion of power over the legislature by the executive remains strong in New Zealand and will not easily change.

8 *Congressional Quarterly's Guide to Congress*, 4th edn, 1991, Washington DC, pp 449–75.

Congressional Standing Committees possess the power to delay or 'kill' Bills before them. New Zealand committees have lost the ability to delay the progress of Bills with the introduction of a six month reporting deadline for Bills. While a Select Committee may recommend that a Bill not proceed, the decision on the future of a Bill ultimately rests with the House.

The Congressional committees may be considered to have more power over and independence from their parent legislature than is the case with their New Zealand counterparts. Congressional committees are even required to produce their own rules and procedures while New Zealand committees are bound by the rules created by the House. New Zealand's more centralised power relationship between the House and its committees may be partially attributed to the smaller size of the legislature. In New Zealand, approximately 95 members currently fill positions on 18 committees and two subcommittees. In the United States, 435 House of Representatives members and 100 Senators fill positions on several hundred Congressional committees and subcommittees.[9] The close, inter-dependent relationship between the New Zealand House of Representatives and its committees is feasible partly because of its small scale.

Recent changes in the balance of power in the US House of Representatives have returned much control to the Speaker. The twentieth century tradition of decentralised, relatively autonomous committees has changed considerably through the consolidation of party position and changes in House procedures to strengthen the influence of the Speaker. Committees have been abolished, lost parts of their jurisdictions, been restricted in the number of subcommittees they may establish or been threatened with these measures. The result has been a reduction in the extent to which committees amend legislation and greater committee compliance in the consideration of legislation. This has been accompanied by a developing trend to challenge the reports of committees in the House.[10]

Some changes in the US House of Representatives bear a resemblance to existing procedures in New Zealand. Greater intervention from party leadership to ensure compliance with their policies is common in New Zealand where government committee chairpersons have frequent contact with ministers. The strict deadlines being imposed on committee consideration of business in the US House follow similar changes in New Zealand.[11] Given the evolving natures of committee systems in New Zealand and the United States, it seems that each system may come to reflect the other

9 *Op cit*, *Congressional Quarterly's Guide to Congress*, fn 8, p 463.

10 Owens, J, *The Return of Party Government in the US House of Representatives: Central Leadership – Committee Relations in the 104th Congress*, 1997, Cambridge, pp 247–57.

11 *Ibid*, p 257.

more closely. However, it is highly unlikely that New Zealand Select Committees will develop greater autonomy from the House of Representatives.

CHAPTER 13

SYSTEM OF COMMITTEES IN THE PARLIAMENT OF SINGAPORE

Heng Chiang Meng, MP, Singapore

It has been the practice of the United Kingdom House of Commons with its membership of about 600 to delegate matters which are complex, technical, detailed or regional to appropriately smaller-sized committees for consideration. These committees, made up of members of the House, vary in size. Some have about five members such as committees deliberating on quasi judicial matters. Others have about 16–50 members, for example, the Estimates Committee; and yet others, the House itself sitting as a Committee of the whole House. Some of the committees in the Commons include the Public Accounts, Estimates, Agriculture, Education and Science, Scottish Grand Committee, etc. Their functions are generally to consider matters referred to them and to report their findings to the House which would then take a final and formal decision.

A similar system of committees also exists in the Singapore Parliament; albeit in a proportionately smaller scale and in much lesser numbers. The Singapore Parliament obviously does not have regional committees such as the Scottish Grand Committee. The largest committee is the whole House sitting in committee. Until recent years, there were only seven committees, excluding the Committee of the whole House. The Standing Orders provide for the Selection, Public Accounts, Estimates, Privileges, Standing Orders, House, and Public Petitions committees. Their functions are similar to the functions of their Commons counterparts. Their membership however ranges from 8 to 10 members.

In addition to these Standing Committees, Standing Orders also provide for the formation of Select Committees of about the same number of members. These committees are set up for scrutinising Bills after the Second Reading and for ad hoc purposes. For example, the eight member Select Committee on the Copyright Bill sat for eight days in 1986 to hear representations and obtain inputs before recommending the copyright code. Recently, a 10 member Select Committee was set up to inquire into the costs of health care in Singapore. The Select Committee on Verification of Health Care Subsidy of Government Polyclinics and Public Hospitals sat through eight sittings, many of which stretched into the night, before coming up with a report which was presented to and accepted by Parliament.

There are also other committees formed either by law or government policy. Under the Constitution, the Committee of Selection will appoint members to a committee for the purpose of nominating membership in

Parliament of Nominated Members of Parliament (NMPs). The ruling People's Action Party (PAP) has also formed the Government Parliamentary Committees, the purpose and functions of which will be mentioned later.

The roles and functions of the various committees in the Singapore Parliament are as follows.

PUBLIC ACCOUNTS COMMITTEE

The Public Accounts Committee has the duty of examining public expenditure. It is a watchdog committee with the task of ensuring that public funds are properly managed and wisely spent. This committee also the powers to examine the accounts of statutory bodies.

ESTIMATES COMMITTEE

The Estimates Committee is another committee which keeps an eye on government expenditures. It studies the estimates of various government and government-related planned expenditure.

STANDING ORDERS COMMITTEE

The Standing Orders Committee reviews from time to time matters relating to the Standing Orders.

HOUSE COMMITTEE

The House Committee considers and advises the Speaker on the comfort and convenience of members of Parliament.

PUBLIC PETITIONS COMMITTEE

Although the Public Petitions Committee will consider all petitions and make its recommendations to Parliament, very few petitions come to Parliament. This is probably because there are other avenues by which citizens could make their grievances heard. This is made easier by the small physical size of Singapore and the fact that an MP would typically be personally involved in constituency functions at least three times in a week, including weekly Meet-the-People sessions (called 'clinics' in the UK).

COMMITTEE OF PRIVILEGES

For obvious reasons, the Committee of Privileges have few opportunities to sit. The Committee deliberates over complaints of breach of privileges and may make punitive recommendations. In a recent case in 1996, the Committee sat to consider the complaint of the Health Minister against a group of representatives for fabricating data and presenting false evidence before the Select Committee on Verification of Health Care Subsidy of Government Polyclinics and Public Hospitals. The Privilege Committee found after conducting a full and thorough inquiry that the representatives were in breach of privileges and recommended that they be fined.

GOVERNMENT PARLIAMENTARY COMMITTEES

A Singaporean innovation to the traditional Westminster committee system was the introduction in 1987 of what is called the Government Parliamentary Committee (GPC) system. The GPCs differ from the conventional Parliamentary Committee as provided for under the Standing Orders of Parliament in that they are government-appointed committees.

When the then First Deputy Prime Minister (DPM), Mr Goh Chok Tong, announced in February 1987 the introduction of the GPCs, he made it clear that the creation of the GPCs would improve the workings of the existing system of parliamentary democracy by enhancing the role of the MPs in the decision making process. Mr Goh also said that the committees would only be credible if they did not appear to collude with the government, the ruling People's Action Party or the civil service. Hence, the GPCs were told to look at issues objectively and independently.

Each GPC would be led by a government backbencher and several other MPs and every GPC will concentrate on specific subjects mirroring those of various government ministries. On the question of whether the GPCs would evolve into Select Committees, Mr Goh said that would depend on the government's experience with them, but for the time being they would remain parliamentary groups formed at the initiative of the governing party.

Since 1987, the GPCs have done a more than creditable job, raising the general standards of debate and making many useful policy suggestions. In 1989, for example, Dr Hong Hai, the then chairman of the Communications and Information GPC, was the first GPC chairman to chair a Select Committee on land transport issues. A number of policy initiatives from the government have since then originated in the GPCs. Giving his first public assessment of the GPCs more than two years after they were formed in 1987, then DPM Mr Goh Chok Tong remarked that:

> The GPCs have worked out well. Debate is more focused. The MPs have more in-depth knowledge of their subject areas. They have also become more assertive as a result. They do not just accept a minister's opinion or judgment. They want to be convinced. So they question and probe. They have raised the quality of debate in Parliament.

It was not surprising then that in early 1991, the government held out the prospects of a more prominent role for the GPCs as Singapore moved into the 21st century.

This has led to suggestions that GPCs should evolve into bipartisan Parliamentary Committees which, like the congressional committees or Parliamentary Committees in Britain, would have the power to summon civil servants and even ministers to testify before them. Such a notion however, has raised fears that the confidentiality and integrity of the civil service could be undermined if MPs have the right to summon civil servants to defend political decisions taken by their ministers.

An event in the later part of 1991 seemed to have caused the government to re-think on the role of the GPCs. In the General Election held in the later part of 1991, the PAP lost four seats to the opposition and the there was also a 2.2 percentage points drop in popular votes compared with 1988. At a post-election conference, Prime Minister (PM) Goh Chok Tong said that GPCs would be removed. With the increase in opposition MPs, there were no necessity for government MPs to raise issues from the platform of GPCs. He added that GPCs would be abolished and PAP MPs would close ranks in the new Parliament. The PAP would revert to the old system of having internal party committees which would discuss issues behind closed doors.

Several weeks later however, PM Goh told reporters that GPCs would continue to function but not in an adversarial manner that would pit PAP backbenchers against their own front bench. Hence, although the fundamental purpose of the GPCs remained the same, its style changed,

Today, there are 11 GPCs in Parliament covering issues like communications, community development, defence and foreign affairs, education, environment, finance and trade and industry, health, home affairs and law, information and the arts, labour and national development. The role of the GPCs today, tempered by the experiences of the initial years, is less confrontational and adversarial. Rather, there is a lot of consultation between the GPC and the ministry concerned on issues of public interest. The GPCs also serve as important sounding boards and provide valuable feedback and suggestions to the ministries concerned. It appears unlikely that the GPCs, at least in the foreseeable future, would evolve into bipartisan Parliamentary Committees.

NATURE OF COMMITTEES

The nature of Parliamentary Committees in Singapore is influenced by the composition of Parliament itself. Because of the small number of opposition MPs, committees have evolved into bodies which receive representations from the public as well as experts. Parliament tries to make each committee as representative as possible by including at least one opposition MP in each committee. Although such procedures tend to make committees mini-chambers, by and large committee sessions tend to be non-partisan, especially on the more complex issues such as trade, company law, etc. However, on political issues, even with one opposition MP, the sessions could be as partisan as committees in other Parliaments.

SIZE OF COMMITTEES

The Standing Orders of Parliament stipulate that the size of the Select Committee should consist of a Chairman and not more than seven other committee members. The relatively small size of the committees make discussions and decision making more manageable. Moreover, the committees and GPCs in Singapore function more like small working groups with certain specific functions. For example the Public Accounts Committee would examine government expenditure, including the accounts of all ministries and statutory boards. The committee would consider the accounts of the Singapore government and statutory boards for any given financial year and also deliberate on the audit findings by the Auditor General in his Report for the financial year. The Auditor General's Report would raise certain matters of concern in the financial control and regulatory environment of the various government ministries, departments and statutory boards. At the end of its deliberation, the committee would issue a report to be presented to Parliament.

The Singapore legislature consists of 83 members. This is relatively small when compared with bigger countries like the UK. Thus, MPs in Singapore sometimes serve in more than one committee. However, its physical size does not preclude the proper functioning of a Parliamentary Committee system and the GPCs. It should also be noted that unlike in many other countries, almost all MPs in Singapore hold full time jobs outside of Parliament which means that they would have less time for Parliamentary Committee work. Thus if committees were like mini-chambers with long-drawn debates, the demand on the time of Singaporean MPs would be onerous. In such a circumstance, then perhaps the Parliamentary Committee system would be operating under greater stress than at present.

A committee system allows the House to refer a particular matter to a committee when it warrants detailed examination, including hearing its views or collecting information on the matter. These tasks are more easily undertaken by a small group of MPs than by the House as a whole. Committees, especially GPCs, also encourage and enable MPs to develop special interests and expertise in particular aspects of public policies. The role of the Parliamentary Committee system is thus closely linked to the effective discharge of Parliament's role as the legislative body of the land. Hence, even for a relatively small legislature like Singapore's, the committee system is still necessary.

FUTURE OF THE COMMITTEE SYSTEM

Modern communication technologies do allow the government to communicate directly to the people. The mass media and the internet have all made communication easier and instantaneous. However, the impact of modern communication technologies does not make the committee system obsolete. Though the government can communicate 'directly' with the people, this does not obviate the role which committees play in a parliamentary democracy. As noted earlier, committees play a pivotal role in dissecting and examining complex pieces of legislation or issues of national importance. More often than not, these legislation and issues of national importance are complex and require a committee to scrutinise, investigate and then present a report to Parliament for deliberation.

As the example of the GPC system in Singapore indicates, the structure of the committee system is not static. Each country would have to improvise in order to make the system of parliamentary democracy suit their particular needs and circumstances. The GPC system was introduced in Singapore so as to enhance the workings of the existing parliamentary system. The GPC was not meant to replace, but rather, to supplement the existing committees provided for under the Standing Orders of Parliament.

In the Singapore context, the committee system is effective, for three strong reasons. First, the committees are not political battlegrounds where politicians fight over personal or partisan agendas. This has helped to ensure that the committees and GPCs carry out their tasks efficiently and expeditiously. Secondly, MPs see their involvement in the committees and GPCs as an important part of their legislative responsibilities and for the newer MPs, a chance to learn about the workings of the highest legislative body of the land. Thirdly, the size of the committees and GPCs make committee work manageable and the tasks allocated are also well defined

There does not appear to be any threat to the future of the committee system. Legislation and issues of national importance are likely to become more complex in a society driven by ever-changing technologies and global considerations. This development itself would mean that committees would be ever more important in helping to scrutinise and dissect complex issues on behalf of the whole chamber.

CONCLUSION

In conclusion, it should be said that the committees have worked well in the Singapore parliamentary context and they are likely to continue performing their vital roles in the foreseeable future. The relatively smaller committee size and the absence of partisan committee politics have ensured the efficiency of these committees in Singapore. This being said, committees in Singapore, as in any other countries, would not remain static. They would have to evolve to suit the changing demands and particular needs of the country. Singapore's innovation with the GPC system and the Nominated MPs are cases in point.

CHAPTER 14

PRIVATE MEMBERS

Hon Dr CT Kuruneri, Zimbabwe

Before delving into the broad question of Private Members' roles in committee work, it is important to give a quick overview of the Select Committee practice in Zimbabwe and, from this review, determine the extent to which:

(a) Private Members are active participants in committee;

(b) Private Members are observers of the clash between experts;

(c) committees are 'make work projects' for Private Members or a place for true consultation with the public between elections';

(d) Private Members express their own private views, the views of the party or the views of their constituencies; and

(e) the whip and party discipline are crystallised within the committee.

SELECT COMMITTEE PRACTICE IN ZIMBABWE

In a parliamentary system of government, Parliament has three principal objectives. These are:

(a) discussion of public affairs;

(b) inquest into administration; and

(c) law making.

However, the enormous range and complexity of legislation and the administrative function of the modern state make it almost impossible for the legislature to adequately fulfil these objectives without imposition of deliberate mechanisms to effect change. While government has vast and highly sophisticated administrative machinery and organisation manned by experts, specialists and seasoned civil servants at its disposal to undertake its complex tasks, Parliament finds itself handicapped in this regard. Through parliamentary devices like questions and debates it is not able to exercise more than sporadic supervision of the administration. In order for Parliament to achieve its objectives to a greater extent and degree than is obtainable in its plenary session, it needs an agency of its own in which the whole House has confidence. This, among other things, Parliament seeks to achieve through Parliamentary Committees composed of a small number of its members.

It is common knowledge that no deliberate or legislative body can conduct its business without having frequently to lead up to and prepare for a final decision by preliminary discussion. Nothing can be more natural than for Parliament to delegate such preliminary work to a body chosen from among its members and of a smaller size than the actual legislative body. Hence the prevalence of committees in Parliament. The Parliament of Zimbabwe, like most Commonwealth Parliaments, possesses an organised system of Select Committees whose aim is to fulfil these objectives.

SELECT COMMITTEES

The nomenclature of the committee system practised in Zimbabwe is inherited from the Westminster model. However, in the United Kingdom House of Commons a distinction is made between standing and Select Committees although both are smaller bodies of the whole House. The Standing Committees in the House of Commons consider principally Public Bills, which are sent to one of them for their committee stage in order that there be thorough examination of the Bill. These Standing Committees are set up afresh with new members for each Bill which is committed to them. In the Parliament of Zimbabwe, there are no Standing Committees. However, there are a number of long-standing Select-Sessional committees appointed or re-appointed sessionally.

The Select-Sessional committees are distinguished from the other *ad hoc* committees as they are concerned with particular subjects, and the procedure to be followed by them is laid down by the Standing Rules and Orders of Parliament. The *ad hoc* Select Committees, on the other hand are established to inquire into and report upon some special matter and are disbanded when their reports are made to the House.

HISTORY OF SELECT COMMITTEE PRACTICE IN ZIMBABWE

The first four Select Committees in the Parliament were appointed in 1924 These were:

(1) Printing Committee;

(2) Standing Rules and Orders Committee;

(3) Library Committee;

(4) Examiner's of Petitions of Private Bills Committee.

However, only the Standing Rules and Orders and the Library Committees have stood the test of time and still exist.

Until the creation of a unicameral Parliament in 1990, there existed eight other Select Committees. These included:

- Internal Arrangements Committee;
- Estimates Committee;
- Pensions and Gratuities Committee;
- Public Accounts Committee;
- Government Assurances Committee.

Since 1980, with the change in the administration and in keeping with the aspirations of a new nation, regular examination has been made to assess the effectiveness of the committee system. It was noted that the Estimates Committee which had a pre-audit function was unable to cope with the volume of work that it was required to do.

The Committee had been established:

> ... to inquire into and report upon such estimates as it may think fit with a view to achieving economies and drawing attention to items which, in the opinion of the committee, may involve or have involved wasteful expenditure in the administration of any ministry or department of government (Old Standing Order 158).

For operational purposes, the committee used to divide itself into two sub-committees in order to cover more ministries in any one session. Even with this arrangement, it became apparent that it was not capable of investigating even half the total number of ministries which it should in any one session.

Based on developments in other Commonwealth Parliaments, a review was carried out in this area and at the end of 1989 the Standing Rules and Orders Committee finally approved a recommendation by staff and introduced a system of Departmental Committees whereby ministries with related functions were placed in four departmental groups. Going by previous experience, it was anticipated that the four Departmental Committees would be capable of carrying out enquiries in at least 16 ministries in any one session, which would be a marked improvement on previous Parliaments. The four Departmental Committees were:

(1) Departmental Committee on Finance, Economic and Development Ministries;

(2) Departmental Committee on Service Ministries;

(3) Departmental Committee on Technical Ministries;

(4) Departmental Committee on Security Ministries.

The scope of the work of these Departmental Committees may be broadly defined as consisting of four types of inquiry, viz:

(a) broad overall review of departments;
(b) review of sections of the departments;
(c) inquiries into problems or aspects of a department's work; and
(d) small 'case' type inquiries into suspected abuses or irregularities.

The establishment of these Departmental Committees led to the abolition of the District Development Fund Estimates Committee, as its requirements were absorbed in the Departmental Committee on Service Ministries. A new Select Committee on Government Assurances was also established, bringing the total to 10. It was also noted that the government business in itself was so demanding for the four departmental committees and suggestions for the setting up of a Committee on Parastatals and State Investments were made and adopted. The terms of reference of the Committee on Parastatals and State Investments are similar to those of the other four departmental committees.

TYPES OF SELECT – SESSIONAL COMMITTEE

The Select Committees of the Parliament of Zimbabwe can be divided into two broad groups – the Watchdog Committees and the Housekeeping Committees. The Watchdog Committees are those that inquire, scrutinise and try to control expenditure.

Watchdog Committees

The following are Watchdog Committees.

Committee on Parastatal and State Investments

This Select Committee with a membership of 11:

> ... inquiries into and reports upon the activities and estimates of expenditure of parastatals and state investments as they think fit with a view to achieving economies and drawing attention to items which, in the opinion of the Committee may involve wasteful or unnecessary expenditure in the administration of any parastatal or state investment.

Since the money invested in parastatals is from the Consolidated Revenue Fund of Zimbabwe, it becomes the responsibility of Parliament to exercise adequate control over its affairs. The committee is, however, barred from examining and investigating matters of major government policy as distinct from business or commercial functions of parastatals or matters of day to day administration or matters for the consideration of which machinery is established by any special statute under which the particular undertaking is established. The examination by the committee is generally in the nature of valuation of the parastatal covering all aspects like production, contribution to the general economy, employment, etc.

Committee on Government Assurances

While replying to questions in the House or during discussions on Bills, Resolutions, etc, ministries often give assurances, promises or undertakings, either to consider a matter or take action or furnish the House with fuller information later. The committee, therefore, scrutinises assurances given by ministries on the floor of the House and reports to the House the extent to which such assurances have been implemented.

The Committee of Government Assurances has a membership of 10 and its chairperson is chosen by the membership of that committee.

Committee on Public Accounts

The Committee of Public Accounts has a membership of 13 and its chairperson is appointed by the Standing Rules and Orders Committee. The chairperson receives a salary in addition to the salary and allowances payable to him as a member.

The Public Accounts Committee examines the accounts showing the appropriation of sums granted by the House for the expenditure of the government in order to ascertain whether the money has been spent as authorised by Parliament and for the purpose for which it was granted.

The committee is interested not merely in discovering technical irregularities, but also in bringing out any evidence of waste, corruption, inefficiency or operational deficiency in the conduct of the nation's financial affairs. It might also record its opinion in the form of disapproval against the extravagance or lack of proper control by the ministry/department.

The committee bases its examination on the audit reports or memoranda of the Comptroller and Auditor General relating to the accounts of the state which are laid before Parliament. The committee is assisted in its work by the Comptroller and Auditor General.

The Committee is not concerned with the question of policy and its findings like any other audit are *ex post facto*.

Housekeeping Committees

On the other hand, the Housekeeping Committees are those whose functions are concerned with powers and procedures of the House or the administration of Parliament.

The following are the Housekeeping Committees.

Standing Rules and Orders Committee

This committee considers and decides upon all matters concerning Parliament. The committee currently has a membership of 15.

Parliamentary Library Committee

The Parliamentary Library Committee looks at matters relating to policy, conduct and management of the Library of Parliament. The committee has a membership of 11.

Pension, Grants and Gratuities Committee

The committee examines and reports upon all minutes and petitions referred to it recommending or preying for pensions, grants and gratuities which are not authorised by law but are in respect of services rendered to the state. The committee has a membership of eight.

Internal Arrangements Committee

This committee looks at and makes recommendations relating to amenities for and conveniences of members. The committee has a membership of 10.

The Committee of Standing Rules and Orders is empowered with the framing of rules that govern the conduct of business of all the Select Sessional Committees. Standing Order No (144i) states that:

> The Standing Rules and Orders Committee shall frame rules relating to the conduct of business in Select Committees. Such Rules, after being laid upon the table of the House, shall continue in force until altered, amended or repealed.

In addition:

> The Select Committee Rules framed by the Standing Rules and Orders Committee in terms of this Standing Order shall have that same force and effect and shall be as binding upon members of Select Committees as are these Standing Orders (144ii).

It is also the Standing Rules and Orders Committee that determines the number and nominates the members to serve on the Select Committees. Currently, the Select Committees membership ranges from eight to 15 with the Standing Rules and Orders Committee having the largest membership.

The chairmen of most Select Committees are appointed by the Standing Rules and Orders Committee.

The first sitting of a Select Committee shall be convened by the Clerk of Parliament within seven days of its constitution. After such a meeting, the chairperson will determine the sittings of the committee. These meetings are held in the Parliament building. However, special permission can be sought from the Speaker for the meeting to be held outside the precincts of Parliament. It is, however, convenient for meetings to be held in Parliament where the secretariat with its staff and equipment, records, paper and precedents, are readily available whenever necessary.

Having decided the course of its proceedings, a Select Committee usually asks for information from government ministries, parastatal bodies, etc. After receiving and considering the information provided, the committee invites witnesses. Witnesses are examined largely from the civil service with the responsible accounting officers being the chief witnesses. Evidence may be taken on oath or affirmation. Questioning is opened by the chairman who then asks members of the committee in turn to put forward their questions.

The Standing Rules specifically provide that the sittings of a committee shall be held in camera. This entails that all proceedings are treated as confidential and it shall not be permissible for a member of the committee or anyone who has access to its proceedings to communicate directly or indirectly, to the press or any one who is not a member of the committee any information regarding its proceedings before it reports to the House. It is only after the report of the committee has been presented to the House that the information can be considered public. Any premature publication or revelation of proceedings of a committee or any part of the report before it is presented to Parliament constitutes a breach of privilege

In a Select Committee meeting, a member can speak more than once on a question under consideration. All questions at any sitting of a committee should be determined by a majority of votes of the members present. In the case of equality of votes, the chairman or the person acting as such will have a second or casting vote.

Select Committees have power to send for persons, papers and records and thus have virtually the same power as a court of law. The power to send for persons extends to anyone from whom the committee wishes to hear evidence. Witnesses invariably attend on receiving a letter from the clerk requesting them to do so. However, although there is a general rule that Select Committees have the power to send for papers and records, it has been left to the consideration of the government to decline to produce a document on the ground that its disclosure would be prejudicial to the 'public interest or the security of the nation'.

The basic idea behind this arises from the fact that, whatever is said in a committee or document that is supplied, will eventually be made public when the committee reports to the House. Therefore, it is necessary to take precautionary measures on issues that are sensitive to state security. In addition, on such issues consultations are held to clarify the government's stand, and to establish a common line of investigation which does not interfere with state security.

Following the taking of evidence, a series of deliberative meetings are held. The chairman, with the help of the committee clerk, prepares a draft report to be circulated and then considered paragraph by paragraph by the committee. Amendments may be moved to it and voted on, as if it were a committee stage of a Bill.

The committee is required to produce only one report to the House. It is the opinion of the committee, not that of individual members, which the House expects, and if there is no unanimity, the conclusions of the majority, are the conclusions of the committee. The one way in which members of the committee can express their dissent from or opposition to the report, or any part of it, is by moving amendments or motions in the committee, and appear as doing so in the minutes of the proceedings.

The final report, when ready, is signed by the chairman and on the resolution of the committee, it is presented to the House. The report is considered by the House only when the chairman or authorised person moves a motion 'That this House takes note of the report of the committee'. The Standing Orders provide that after a period of debate of 21 sitting days, the minister is supposed to respond, giving some indication of what action the government has taken or whether they will consider adopting any of the recommendations. However, in reality, ministers take their time to respond to these reports. This has led most backbenchers to question whether the government takes Parliament reports seriously.

As the Select Committee has no executive powers and simply performs the task imposed upon it and submits its report to the House, it cannot guarantee that any action will be taken or give direct orders that something it thinks desirable be done. The House itself cannot guarantee that the recommendations of the committee are adopted by the concerned ministry. The main reason lies in the relationship between Parliament and the Executive. While the function of Parliament is principally to enact legislation, authorising the raising of revenue and control government expenditure, it is the function of the Executive to carry out the duties of the State, such as deciding policy and executing it in any way it sees fit.

STAFFING

The committees are manned by a committee clerk who is asked to:

- give procedural advice to the committee;
- take minutes of the committee meetings;
- receive and store documents on behalf of the committee; and
- carry out all administrative duties for the committee.

In order to perform these duties, the clerk has to be an expert in that line of work. The clerk must have thorough knowledge of the relevant rules and a clear grasp of the intricacies and nuances of procedures.

ROLE OF PRIVATE MEMBERS IN COMMITTEE

The Oxford dictionary defines 'role' as:

(1) an actors part; and

(2) a persons or things function.

It also defines 'active' as:

(1) taking part in activities; and

(2) having an effect (among other things).

For a Private Member to play a role and/or an active role in committee presupposes that he or she understands the issues, the subject matter and has volumes of information at his/her disposal to make an informed decision. Where information is not readily available, the ability to play a role and especially an active role is immediately compromised. It, therefore, follows that the starting point in anyone's participation in committee work is information. Are Private Members active participants in committee? The answer is plain and simple. They are participants only to the extent that they have accurate information and are able to use it.

The issue of Private Members being observers of the clash between experts is redundant. Where you have experts and non-experts, it follows that someone will be a spectator or, at best, a good listener.

Are committees a medium for 'make work projects' for Private Members or a place for true consultation with the public between elections? This particular question needs to be properly focused. We noted in our introduction that the enormous range and complexity of legislation and the administrative function of the modern state makes it impossible for the legislature to adequately implement its three principal objectives of discussing public affairs, inquiring into the administrative function, as well as making laws. We also noted that, for this reason, there is a requirement to impose a deliberate mechanism to assist in the fulfilment of Parliament's objectives, and that this mechanism is in the form of Parliamentary Committees.

It follows, therefore, that the only way committees can be a medium for 'make work projects', is if they are allowed to do so. Here, both the chairmen of committees and indeed the Speaker can act as safeguards pre-empting this type of practice depending, of course, on what system is in place. If the approach is both purposeful and purposive, the likelihood of abuse is non-existent and committee activity could be a true medium for effective consultation with the public between elections.

The matter of Private Members expressing their own private views, the view of the party, and the views of their constituencies depends critically on how the actual political system is organised, structured and administered. It also depends on what range of views one has in mind. If one were referring to issues of inflation, the need to subsidise interest rates, terms of trade, unemployment, drought or the need to raise salaries for civil servants, one's ability to hold views would depend critically on one's ability to articulate the same or to have an ability to consult where certain information is lacking. Here, it must be said that the ability to raise questions has, obviously, a positive correlation with ability to understand the subject matter. There must be a logical expectation of likely outcome otherwise questions become meaningless. I am saying this fully aware that there are issues of value judgments here. But then, these are unavoidable whenever issues of politics, party and policy are involved.

The matter of constituency views is a slightly easier one to deal with. Here, what matters is the Private Member's ability to grasp the pertinent issues affecting his/her constituency and the relevance of the debate at hand in addressing those issues. These the Private Member is given, perhaps after seeking them out. The depth of argument behind them requires, obviously, that the Private Member, from his own point of view, be well informed and/or schooled on the main ingredients of the subject and argument.

The extent to which the role of the whip and party discipline are crystallised within the committee depends on a variety of factors:

(a) the representation of the various parties in the committee;

(b) the political system, structure and organisation of Parliament itself;

(c) the political acumen of the whip; and

(d) the relationship between the chairmen of the various committees and the whip.

Where one party enjoys a dominant majority in Parliament, it follows that the said party's views will determine the direction of things – but, here one has to be quick to say that the determination of direction will also have something to do with the political system structure, and the organisation of Parliament itself. If the whip is particularly skilled and experienced, and his party has an absolute majority in Parliament, it also follows that he is likely to have reasonable chances of getting his party's way through the committee system.

Committee work has a direct and positive correlation with the calibre of the Private Members in question. Where the system is dominated by low calibre members, there will be low productivity. Where there are high calibre members, the opposite holds, and, of course, this brings one to the whole ticklish issue of the selection of Private Members and the electioneering process practised by different democracies.

And this is where our initial and long term problem begins. If we accept that the issues of democracy and human rights are inseparable, we must also allow ourselves to be bound by them for better or worse. Democracy has been described as the rule by the majority over the minority. And, in a modern State, we also accept that the most fundamental of human rights is one's right to vote or to select (the famous universal adult suffrage). The question to ask is whether in order to exercise one's democratic and human rights function, it follows that:

(a) an 'ignorant' majority should vote or make a selection?;

(b) the majority view, regardless of its content, prevail?;

(c) criteria should not be set to determine minimum selection requirements for Private Members during primary elections?

These are ticklish questions and one hopes that this conference will be able to shed some light on them from the many experiences that are shared here. With this brief theoretical background I now wish to turn to how this all fits into the Zimbabwean context.

INFORMATION

Up until very recently, the Parliament of Zimbabwe Library and available research facilities were inadequate in fulfilling the information requirements for Private Members. Consequently, debate in the house was largely uninformed, boring, shallow and misleading. The problem did not only emanate here. The Zimbabwean Central Statistical Office itself is inadequately equipped and is, therefore, not producing data on time, let alone effective and accurate data. The Private Member is only as effective as the data and information available to him/her. In committee work, this particular constraint has some rather devastating effects.

It is the source of emotional but uninformed arguments by some members leading to some chairman having to run tutorials prior to dealing with the main subject of investigation. Committee work is not completed on time as most work ends up being done by the chairman and the committee clerk.

Some Private Members seem to come to committee largely to collect their sitting allowances and occasionally to escape the 'heated family environment'. As a result, Parliament's effectiveness in discussing public affairs, inquire into the administrative function and to make laws is compromised. However, with Parliament now on the internet it is hoped that our library and research assistants can now deliver useful information and data to Private Members, and that this should lead to improvement in debate and other contributions by Private Members.

EXPERTS AND OUTSIDE CONTRIBUTIONS

The current structure of the Zimbabwe Parliament's committee system does not have provision for public participation. As a result, the chances of Private Members being observers of the clash between experts are largely reduced if not eliminated. Committees can, however, invite expertise from outside to make contributions in camera. It is the responsibility of the chairman to ensure that reasonable scope is developed to allow all members to participate. This is often achieved through prepared questions that Private Members are given to ask, taking turns in doing so.

However, although this arrangement works well with the initial prepared questions, it can be a disaster when it comes to supplementaries. It should be noted that the Private Members' ability to continue with questions presupposes a certain depth of knowledge in the subject matter. Where this depth is not there, and, in the absence of an astute chairman and committee clerk, certain embarrassment has been registered.

But, with an effective chairman and regular consultation with Mr Speaker, some of these problems can be avoided and Parliament's ability to tap usable information from experts enhanced. As well, the chances for committees being a medium for 'make work projects' in Zimbabwe are very, slim. This is largely because of the type and clarity of problems that confront us. The 'make work projects' syndrome works where projects' requirements are dubious.

In the Zimbabwean context, committees have so far done an excellent job in project selection. Where there are constraints is after the work has been done and findings and recommendations are tabled in the House. Here, there is no mechanism to make Ministries or the government implement the recommendations and decisions of the committees and indeed of Parliament. Consequently, Private Members often find themselves frustrated and discouraged as many months of work translate into dust in the Parliament Library.

Zimbabwe, while an obvious democracy, also possesses a very unique character. The Parliament is largely dominated by one party, ZANU PF. Out of total membership of 150, only three are from the opposition and/or independents. Here, it follows that the views and especially the political views that carry the day in committee work, are those of the ruling party. Here, emphasis is on political views rather than technical views. The exercise of technical view is a matter of the calibre of the Private Member and/or their ability to do research regardless of party. In such a situation, the whip can literally go on safari and not expect party principles and discipline to be compromised unless, of course, there is a matter of gross misrepresentation. In the absence of the latter, committee chairmen and the whip are safely confirmed in the driver's seat with regard to future direction or orientation.

EFFECTIVENESS OF THE COMMITTEE SYSTEM AND PRIVATE MEMBERS

If Private Members in committee are to achieve maximum effectiveness, it is important that their recommendations receive wide publicity and concern. The publicity would lead to the formation of public opinion which would exert considerable pressure on the government to act upon constructive and practical suggestions. Committee recommendations can, however, be implemented without publicity and the government should be encouraged to pay greater attention and respect to the views of the committees.

Generally, Select Committees do not concern themselves with policy. Some Select Committees, like the Public Accounts Committee, only determine whether money has been appropriately disbursed for the attainment of set political goals, but do not determine or question whether these objectives are desirable. In such circumstances the committee cannot recommend for the alteration of policy on which the expenditure is based. The Private Members' lack of involvement in policy considerations greatly reduce their effectiveness in committee and to a certain extent, renders their involvement meaningless.

The terms of reference of some Select Committees make them quite ineffective. For example, the Committee on Government Assurances is expected to 'keep track of all assurances, promises and undertakings given by the government on the floor of the House'. They do not give any indication whether there is a set period of time when government is supposed to report on any undertaking.

However, unless an assurance is implemented within a reasonable time, its purpose and value is lost. As the terms are now constituted, the Committee does not have any power to push the government to implement the assurances. Naturally, the Committee, being an advisory body of the House, would not force the government to act within a specified time. However, it would tremendously strengthen the executive's accountability to the legislature if the Committee's role went beyond that of 'advisory body'.

Select Committees, as presently constituted, cannot investigate Bills even when they relate to the ministry being investigated or regardless of whether such Bills will impact on the overall expenditure the ministry. This is largely related to the Parliament's limited role in policy formulation.

PUBLIC PARTICIPATION IN COMMITTEES

The committee system can be greatly improved and will make Parliament more relevant and effective by allowing participation of the public and experts on specific subjects. This will automatically lead to the falling off of the requirement that all committee meetings should be held in camera. The introduction of public hearings, will enhance public participation in parliamentary issues and enhance the awareness and general knowledge of Private Members.

CONCLUSION

The value of Parliamentary Select Committees and the role of Private Members cannot be overstated. Through committees, Parliament does not only learn about the nature of problems dealt with by individual ministries and other government organisations, it is also afforded an opportunity to scrutinise government activities thereby strengthen accountability to Parliament. It should however be noted that committees can neither give directives to a minister nor officials. All they do is to draw attention to what they consider to be problems or make recommendations for the consideration of the minister and his officials. The Private Member has the responsibility to be informed. Here, the calibre of the Private Member is critical. However, it goes without saying that, as long as Parliament's ability to provide basic information to Private Members is compromised, no meaningful contribution will be forthcoming in committee or in the whole House.

CHAPTER 15

NOTES REGARDING REPORT STAGE

Desmond Leakey, MP, Jamaica

I am requested to comment on the Report Stage of Committees as these Reports relate to:

(a) the relationship of the committee to the executive;

(b) is the government listening?;

(c) are there procedures that can be followed if a committee report is being ignored?;

(d) can or should a committee force the government's agenda?;

(e) involvement of the media at report stage;

(f) should a committee help the government lead or follow public opinion?

The fundamental principle underpinning the Westminster parliamentary democracy is the delegation of responsibility for policy to a Cabinet of which the majority are members of Parliament. In the case of political plurality, the question of policy is even more restricted to the Cabinet since any divergence from policy may be interpreted as an emergence of division in the party.

Now, because the Westminster model is practised by most Parliaments in the Commonwealth, we have come to regard the Cabinet as the focal point of the decision making process of government and we are not unmindful of the relationship between Cabinet and Parliament.

The selection of Cabinets in the Westminster model is usually the exclusive prerogative of the Prime Minister, and thereafter Cabinet members invariably become beholden to offer a loyalty to the government and avoid any strong divergence in views.

New members of Parliament usually maintain a closer link to their constituents and the wider society and are usually placed in a position to interpret the impact (negatively or positively) of the policies implemented by the government. Traditionally, they are limited in making their point of view known.

The avenue of the party structure is usually limited in scope because of how the party machinery is structured and functions. The regular debates in Parliament are under some constraints and are limited in scope by decisions previously taken in caucus.

Consequently, the Parliamentary Committee and the scope to investigate and hold hearings on issues must in its reporting mechanism have the capacity to influence the government.

However, the reality is that most decisions of government are made by Cabinet, but can only be implemented after they have been approved by Parliament.

The committee is presently appointed by the Parliament on the recommendation of the executive through the Leader of Government Business in Parliament. This procedure of appointment sets the stage of responsibility to government especially since in making the recommendations on membership, the chairmanship is included.

The committee by practice must be seen as independent of the government and, therefore, the mechanism of selecting the committee should employ a wider democratic process within the majority parliamentary groupings. The alternative could be that:

(a) the group recommends the membership of the committee;

(b) the committee when appointed selects its chairman.

This would establish a level of independence from the executive. (This could be limited to perception only.)

Having identified Cabinet as the focal point from where decisions flow – and the body which receives information to assist and facilitate the making of decisions, and it can stand repetition that Cabinet is the dominant force in the executive government of most, if not all, of the Commonwealth countries – so, the question: is the government listening? I think the answer is 'yes'. One of the outstanding and certainly enduring features of parliamentary democracy inherited and practised by the exponents of the Westminster model is the political neutrality and independence of the executive. It does not belong to any party. As individuals, those serving as members do have their own political views, but those of us who have been exposed to the system find that, when it comes to performing their public duties, individual members of the executive are usually neutral and objective. They do listen.

There is some evidence in the Jamaican experience which indicate that the government is responsive to the findings and recommendations of the committees.

On the question of whether a committee should force the government's agenda, in this connection, it might be interesting to note certain developments which took place in Jamaica during the last Session of Parliament. One of my colleagues, Mr Sam Lawrence, the member for Portland Eastern, successfully brought a motion to the House recommending an amendment to the Standing Orders in the following terms:

> (1) Every Private Members' motion carried by the House which requires action on national policy issues or constituency representational issues shall

stand referred to the Select Committee whose terms of reference relate to the subject matter of the motion, for the question of the appropriateness of the subject for submission to the Cabinet to be considered, and the Committee shall submit its report thereon within 14 days of the referral of the motion.

(2) If consequent on a referral pursuant to paragraph (1) the relevant Select Committee approves the preparation of a submission to the Cabinet then the leader of Government Business in the House, subject to the approval of the House, shall within 21 days of the tabling of such approval make a submission to Cabinet inviting their consideration of the subject matter of the motion as approved by the House.

(3) A Cabinet decision in response to a submission made pursuant to paragraph (2) shall be tabled in the House not later than 21 days after being made.

The motion was referred to the Standing Orders Committee. The Committee accepted the recommendation, and the terms contained in the amendment, now forms a part of the procedure of the House.

With reference to the involvement of the media, I will also attempt to address the issue by outlining certain developments in the Jamaica Parliament which occurred as I recall in 1991, where the Standing Orders were amended to enable all meetings of Select Committees to be held in public. The only exception is the Standing Finance Committee of the whole House on the Estimates of Expenditure.

The Standing Orders were also amended to delete the section dealing with 'Premature publication of evidence' which read as follows:

Premature publication of evidence

The proceedings of and the evidence taken before any Select Committee and any documents presented to and decisions of such a committee shall not be published by any member thereof or by any other person before the committee have presented their report to the House.

This section was amended in the following terms:

Premature publication of evidence

When evidence has been given before a Select Committee meeting in public, no complaint of privilege will be entertained on the ground that it has been published before having been reported to the House.

This amendment as you will appreciate clearly removes the threat of any person or persons being in breach of privilege, of whom the most likely 'offender' would be the media.

There is absolutely no doubt that where the weaknesses of a ministry or department are questioned and thoroughly investigated in a committee, that the impact is certainly more pronounced than when these matters are dealt with on the floor of the House by way of debate or at question time, so by the in-depth exposure, aided by the ability to cross examine persons, and if this is further assisted by ample coverage by the media, it would certainly have the effect of mobilizing public opinion, and as a consequence act as a sounding board, thereby giving government an opportunity to take note of public opinion, and this should ultimately assist in its leadership role.

In conclusion, I think it is true to say that the relationship of the committee to the executive is usually one of mutual respect. In my own experience, committee reports are not being ignored. I think a committee should attempt to persuade, not force, the government's agenda. The reservation of the government to amend and adjust recommendations especially without reference to the committee has a potential to reduce the effectiveness of the committee and the participation of members, especially when such adjustments unduly change the substance of the recommendations and what they set out to achieve. There are mechanism by way of Standing Orders to get a timely response but no guarantee that the result will reflect the position of the committee. (See Appendix I, p 87.)

The involvement of the Press, often referred to as the fourth estate, is very vital to the democratic process and this involvement should certainly be encouraged.

REPORT OF THE STANDING ORDERS COMMITTEE OF THE HOUSE OF REPRESENTATIVES ON THE RESOLUTIONS TO AMEND SECTION OF THE STANDING ORDERS OF THE HOUSE OF REPRESENTATIVES

Members of this Honourable House are reminded that, on 24 October 1995, the House of Representatives, by Resolution moved by the leader of the House for the adoption of the Report of the Standing Orders Committee which was laid in the House on 27 June 1995, recommitted the Report to the Standing Orders Committee for reference to the Attorney General and the Chief Parliamentary Counsel for examination, comment and final drafting.

At a subsequent meeting held on 28 March 1996, the Committee requested that the decisions taken with respect to the proposed amendments to the Standing Orders of this Honourable House be communicated to the Chief Parliamentary Counsel for consideration and appropriate action.

The redrafted amendments submitted by the Chief Parliamentary Counsel were subsequently considered by the Committee at its Meetings convened on 10, 15 and 24 October 1996, at which time the Committee made certain modifications to these amendments.

The Committee also requested that the modifications agreed upon by the Members, subject to consultations with the Chief Parliamentary Counsel, be included in the final Report to be laid before this Honourable House for adoption.

The Committee has the honour to recommend the following amendments:

New Standing Order No 11A

Insert immediately after Standing Order No. 11 the following heading and entry as Standing Order No 11A:

'Statements by ministers

11A Contents of statement

A statement by a minister shall be limited to matters which directly relate to the subject or department with the responsibility for which he has been charged or which are of urgent national importance.'

Standing Order No 15

1 Delete from paragraph (3) all the words appearing after the word 'asterisk' and substitute therefor the following:

'and a question not so marked shall require a written answer, which when received shall be circulated with the Minutes of the proceedings of the House.'

2 Insert the following as paragraphs (4) and (5):

'(4) Subject to paragraph (5) a question marked for oral answer shall be put down for a day to be named by the member being a sitting day of the House not earlier than 21 clear days after the question has appeared on the Question Paper.

(5) Where a question for oral answer is asked of:

(a) the Prime Minister, in relation to a matter of national importance and national interest; or

(b) a minister, in relation to a matter directly related to his portfolio responsibility, which is of urgent national importance. It shall be put down for a day not earlier than seven clear days after it has been handed to the Clerk.'

Standing Order No 17

Insert in paragraph (5) immediately after the word 'House' the words 'in accordance with Standing Order No 17A'.

New Standing Orders Nos 17A, 17B and 17C

Insert immediately after Standing Order No 17 the following as Standing Orders Nos 17A, 17B and 17C:

'17A Deferral of question

(1) A minister seeking to defer answering a question shall hand to the Clerk a written request therefor which explains the reasons why the answer could not be supplied in the time required and if the House is satisfied with the explanation, the House may extend the time for answering by a period of not more than 14 clear days.

(2) The procedure specified in paragraph (1) shall apply to any further extension required by the minister so, however, that in such case consent to such extension and the length thereof shall be obtained from the Speaker and the questioning member. However, if there is no agreement between the Speaker and the member, the matter shall be determined by the ruling of the Speaker.

(3) Where an answer to the question has not been supplied within the time required under paragraph (2) this shall, subject to any recommendation to the contrary on reference to the Committee of Privileges, be regarded as being out of order.

17B Prime Minister's Question Time

During the second sitting of the House in each month, there shall be a Question Time during which responses by the Prime Minister to questions asked of him in relation to matters of national importance and national interest shall take precedence.

17C Minister's Question Time

On the first sitting day of the House during any week, there shall be a Question Time during which responses by ministers to questions in relation to matters of urgent national importance directly related to their respective portfolio responsibilities shall take precedence.'

Standing Order No 23

Standing Order No 23 is hereby amended in paragraph (2) by adding thereto immediately after the words 'Order Paper' the words 'and not later than 21 days after the date of such first publication'.

New Standing Order 26A

Insert immediately after Standing Order No. 26 the following as Standing Order No 26A:

'26A Motions on national or constituency issues:

(1) Every Private Members' motion carried by the House which requires action on national policy issues or constituency representational issues shall stand referred to the Select Committee whose terms of reference relate to the subject matter of the motion, for the question of the appropriateness of the subject for submission to the Cabinet to be considered, and the committee shall submit its report thereon within fourteen days of the referral of the motion.

(2) If consequent on a referral pursuant to paragraph (1) the relevant Select Committee approves the preparation of a submission to the Cabinet then the leader of government business in the House, subject to the approval of the House, shall within 21 days of the tabling of such approval make a submission to Cabinet inviting their consideration of the subject matter of the motion as approved by the House.

(3) A Cabinet decision in response to a submission made pursuant to paragraph (2) shall be tabled in the House not later than 21 days after being made.'

Standing Order No 68

Standing Order No 68 is hereby amended:

(a) by inserting in paragraph (1) immediately after sub-paragraph (e) the following as sub-paragraphs (f), (g), (h), (i) and (j):

'(f) the Public Administration and Appropriations Committee;

(g) the Internal and External Affairs Committee;

(h) the Economy and Production Committee;

(i) the Human Resource and Social Development Committee;

(j) the Infrastructure and Physical Development Committee;'

[See, also, Appendix II, p 92.]

(b) by deleting paragraph (3) and substituting therefor the following:

'(3) Subject to the provisions of Standing Order No 71, a Sessional Select Committee shall consist of not less than six members, including the chairman, none of whom shall be a minister or parliamentary Secretary.'

New Standing Orders Nos 73A, 73B and 73C

Insert immediately after Standing Order 73 the following as Standing Orders Nos 73A, 73B and 73C:

73A The Public Administration and Appropriations Committee

The Public Administration and Appropriations Committee shall have the duty of:

(a) examining budgetary expenditure of government agencies to ensure that expenditure is done in accordance with parliamentary approval;

(b) monitoring expenditure as it occurs and keeping the Parliament informed of how the Budget is being implemented; and

(c) inquiring into the administration of the government to determine hindrances to efficiency and to make recommendations to the government for improvement of public administration.

73B The Internal and External Affairs Committee

The Internal and External Affairs Committee shall have the duty of:

(a) examining all matters relating to the foreign policy of the government, and analysing the implications and likely effect thereof on Jamaica; and

(b) examining treaties and other international agreements and advising the Parliament of their likely impact on Jamaica; and

(c) examining matters relating to national security and the administration of justice and making recommendations to the Parliament thereon.

73C The Economy and Production, Human Resources and Social Development, and Infrastructure and Physical Development Committees

Each of the Committees established under paragraphs (h), (i) and (j) of Standing Order No 68 shall have terms of reference in relation to the subject matter Indicated by its designation and accordingly shall have the duty of:

(a) examining policy documents and statements from ministries and government agencies which have a bearing on the subject matter of its terms of reference;

(b) examining legislative proposals which may have an effect on the subject matter of its terms of reference and making recommendations to the Cabinet through the Legislation Committee;

(c) receiving submissions from citizens and organizing meetings between citizens, community groups, sectoral organizations, members of Parliament and representatives of government agencies to facilitate exchange of views on the operations of the government and their effect on communities and groups in the society; and

(d) organizing meetings with relevant organizations in order to seek such Information on their activities as the public interest may demand.'

New Standing Order No 77

Insert immediately after Standing Order No 77 the following as Standing Order No 77A:

'77A Referral of matters to Select Committee

A matter may be referred to a Select Committee if, on the question being put, at least 16 members of the House so decide.'

THE ECONOMY AND PRODUCTION, HUMAN RESOURCES AND SOCIAL DEVELOPMENT, AND INFRASTRUCTURE AND PHYSICAL DEVELOPMENT COMMITTEES

Each of the committees established under paragraphs (h), (i) and (j) of Standing Order No 68 shall have terms of reference in relation to the subject matter indicated by its designation and accordingly shall have the duty of:

(a) examining policy documents and statements from ministries and government agencies which have a bearing on the subject matter of its terms of reference;

(b) examining legislative proposals which may have an effect on the subject matter of its terms of reference and making recommendations to the Cabinet through the Legislation Committee;

(c) receiving submissions from citizens and organizing meetings between citizens, community groups sectoral organizations, members of Parliament and representatives of government agencies to facilitate exchange of views on the operations of the government and their effect on communities and groups in the society; and

(d) organizing meetings with relevant organizations in order to seek such information on their activities as the public interest may demand.

CHAPTER 16

GENERAL OVERVIEW OF THE STRUCTURE AND FUNCTIONING OF COMMITTEES OF THE JAMAICAN PARLIAMENT

Desmond Leakey, MP, Jamaica

PURPOSE, FUNCTION AND OPERATION

The Standing Orders of the House of Representatives makes provision for the appointment of Sessional Select Committees which last for an entire Session and Special Select Committees which may or may not last for the entire Session. The functions of Sessional Select Committees are specified in the Standing Orders while the Special Select Committees are given their terms of reference by the House on appointment.

These committees, with the exception of the Standing Orders and the House Committees, have the power to send for persons, papers, and records. All committees of Parliament, with the exception of the Standing Finance Committee, are open to the public, including the media. The media are, therefore, free to report on the proceedings. If matters to be discussed are of a confidential nature these may be discussed by a sub-committee, at the relevant ministry, without the media being present, or discussed with the chairman only.

TYPES OF COMMITTEES

Committee of the whole House

The only committee of the whole House is the Standing Finance Committee, which has responsibility for examining the Estimates of Expenditure in detail. This Committee is not open to the media. It can recommend increases or decreases in the various heeds of expenditure or adoption of the Estimates without amendment.

After second reading of a Bill, it is committed to a committee of the whole House for clause by clause analysis.

Sessional Committees

The following are the Sessional Select Committees which last for an entire session. They may be regarded as Standing Committees.

Public Accounts Committee

This Committee is responsible for examining the accounts of government departments to ensure that public funds are properly spent. Generally, it examines the report of the Auditor General and seeks explanations from relevant officers regarding expenditure or incorrect procedures. This committee is chaired by the opposition and meets once per week.

Standing Orders Committee

This Committee considers matters relating to the Standing Orders which may be referred by the House. It can recommend changes in the Standing Orders.

House Committee

This Committee meets when required. Its function is to advise the Speaker on all matters connected to the comfort and convenience of Members of the House.

Committee on Privileges

This Committee deals with matters referred to it by the House which affect the powers or privileges of the House.

Regulations Committee

This Committee has the responsibility of examining all such Regulations, as under the authority of any Act are to be laid before the House, and to be subject to negative resolution.

Economy and Production Committee

Human Resource and Social Development Committee

Infrastructure and Physical Development Committee

These three oversight Committees are charged with the responsibility of:

(a) examining policy documents and statements from ministries and government agencies which have a bearing on the subject matter of its terms of reference;

(b) examining legislative proposals which may have an effect on the subject matter of its terms of reference;

(c) receiving submissions from citizens and organizing meetings between citizens community groups, sectoral organizations, members of Parliament and representatives of government agencies to facilitate exchange of views on the operations of government and their effect on communities and groups in the society;

(d) organizing meetings with relevant organizations in order to seek such information on their activities as the public interest may demand.

There are two other oversight committees:

(1) The Public Administration and Appropriations Committee with responsibility for:

  (a) examining budgetary expenditure of government agencies to ensure that expenditure is done in accordance with parliamentary approval;

  (b) monitoring expenditure as it occurs and keeping Parliament informed of how the budget is being implemented;

  (c) inquiring into the administration of government and determining hindrances to efficiency and making recommendations to government for improvement of public administration.

(2) The Internal and External Affairs Committee with responsibility for:

  (a) examining all matters relating to the foreign policy of the government and analysing the implications and likely effect thereof on Jamaica;

  (b) examining treaties and other international agreements and advising Parliament on their likely impact on Jamaica.

  (c) examining matters relating to national security and the administration of justice and making recommendations to the Parliament thereon.

Legislative Committees

In addition to the Standing Oversight Committees and other Sessional Select Committees, from time to time, Special Select Committees or Joint Select Committees (from both Houses) are appointed to examine and report on Bills. Through these committees, the public is afforded an input into the determination of legislation.

Special Committees

Sometimes Special or Joint Select Committees may be formed to examine and report on Reports which have been tabled in Parliament. Parliamentary committees cannot take the place of judicial inquiries.

Size of committees

A Sessional Select Committee can have no less than six members, and must reflect the composition of Parliament.

Witnesses

All Select Committees with the exception of the Standing Orders and House Committees have the power to send for persons, papers and records. Witnesses may be summoned by the Clerk on behalf of the House.

A committee usually invites witnesses whom it feels can contribute to the subject matter under discussion. Sometimes, notices are placed in the media inviting interested persons to make written submissions to the committee. The committee then decides which, if any of those persons who made submissions, it wishes to hear.

With the exception of the Standing Finance Committee, ministers are rarely called to give evidence before a committee.

Selection of chairman

The Standing Orders of the House stipulates who should be chairman for some committees. For example, the Speaker is designated as chairman of the Standing Orders Committee and the Committee of Privileges; the Leader of the House is chairman of the House Committee.

Although the Standing Orders provide that other Select Committees may elect their own chairman, the chairman is usually identified by the House.

With the exception of the Public Accounts Committee which is chaired by the opposition, and those previously mentioned which are chaired by the Leader of the House or the Speaker, all other committees are chaired by the government members. With respect to the oversight committees, the chairman decides on the subject matter to be dealt with, and indicates relevant persons/organizations who should attend the various sittings to give evidence. The chairperson is not in training for Cabinet or the Speakership. He functions more as the leader of the inquiry rather than a neutral party.

Staff and facilities for committees

The current facilities are limited in terms of meeting rooms and staffing. The committees are directly serviced by the committee co-ordinator and two research officers. Support is also provided by the clerk and deputy clerk to the Houses. Witnesses are questioned by the members of the committee including the chairman.

Outside advisors and experts are also invited to give evidence or to research topics and present papers.

The Standing Orders provide that:

> ... the chairman of a Select Committee shall prepare a draft report and submit it for consideration of the committee but alternative drafts may be submitted for consideration by any other member of the committee.

In practice, however, the draft report is prepared by the committee co-ordinator, or the research officers, or the chairman may have it prepared by a consultant. The committee members would then determine the final document.

The costs associated with the work of the committees are included in the budget of the Houses of Parliament for which the Clerk to the Houses is the accounting officer.

Private Members

Private Members are active participants in the committees. The committees are true fora for consultations with the public on various issues.

CHAPTER 17

WITNESSES

Senator David MacGibbon, Australia

INTRODUCTION

Witnesses are one of the most valuable tools available to any legislature and its committees. In general terms, witnesses can be viewed as a primary source of information, as a mirror on the views of the community or sector which they represent, as a means of providing feedback on the validity or otherwise of an action or a policy and, finally, they are a tangible example of the desire to achieve transparency or otherwise in the decision making process.

In the Australian Senate, witnesses are usually regarded both as a source of information and explication of government policy – public service and ministerial witnesses – and, frequently, as an alternative to the government view – individuals, lobby groups and professional bodies. All witnesses, whether public service, ministerial or individuals and associations, appearing before committees inevitably have an axe to grind, and it is through the weighing of their alternative views of policy, and the sifting and evaluation of factual information on which those policies are based, that a Parliamentary Committee can make sound and considered recommendations to the legislature.

Given the generally positive nature of Senate Committee dealings with witnesses, it is therefore interesting to me, as a long standing member of committees of inquiry since I came to the Senate in 1978, that the suggested headings under which I have been asked to address this conference are primarily defensive and adversarial.

It concerns me that too much emphasis is often placed on the punitive and regulatory aspects of parliamentary proceedings, rather than on the positive relationship that Parliaments and their committees should, and normally do, have with their constituencies and sources of advice. Because of this positive element, the standing of Parliament has been enhanced. While it is true that committees inquiring into activities of government, such as our Estimates Committees, which deal with the appropriation of money for the various departments of State, often have to struggle to extract the relevant information from public servants imbued, quite mistakenly, with the code of silence, that is not the general rule.

Members of Parliament always have an open door for their individual constituents and groups within their electorate. But, in one sense, this is a private relationship. Parliamentary Committees through their public hearings and subsequent reports provide a very good and very important human link between what is often seen as an impersonal and remote Parliament and the people.

The letter of invitation in relation to witnesses sets out six points to be specifically addressed. This paper will commence with a resumé of the procedures adopted in the Australian Senate in relation to witnesses and will be a general discussion. The specific points will then follow.

The Privilege Resolutions of the Senate, particularly Resolution No 1, deal with the protection of witnesses. The use of the word protection is intentional. This resolution forms Appendix I, p 110 to this chapter.

PRIVILEGE RESOLUTION 1

Resolution regulates committee behaviour

The purpose of the resolution, which was codified early in 1988, but did in fact represent long standing Senate practice, was to bind the committees in their dealings with their valuable resource, witnesses, rather than using sanctions against witnesses in their dealings with committees.

Invitations, not summonses, to witnesses

It is the experience of the Senate that the normal processes of dealing with witnesses are not adversarial or antagonistic but 'inquisitive' in the proper sense of that word. Thus, in the normal course of events and as indicated by paragraph (1) of the Privilege Resolution, committees are enjoined to invite a witness to attend a committee meeting to give evidence. Naturally, committees are also given the power to summon witnesses, but only when a deliberate decision has been made that the circumstances so warrant. Circumstances which might warrant such a decision could be that a committee feared that a person might leave the country or otherwise escape its jurisdiction. These are so extreme that I can think of only two or three instances where summoning on these grounds has been undertaken.

A more interesting use of this power has been a form of 'protective' summons, where a witness has asked a committee to issue a summons, so that that witness can explain to the powers-that-be in an organization that he/she is required to appear. Although committees have made it clear that witnesses are afforded all the protections that a House of Parliament can accord as a result of responding to an invitation, a summons under these circumstances has been a form of reassurance to a witness that a committee has been willing to give.

Similar provisions and protections apply in respect of the production of documents (paragraph (2)).

Natural justice provisions of the resolution

Paragraphs (3) and (4) – reasonable notice to appear and opportunity to make written submissions – are, in effect, natural justice provisions. Given, however, that most committee hearings are cooperative ventures, and that sometimes the Senate demands from the committees a very fast turnaround time between receiving the reference and reporting to the Senate, both committees and witnesses are frequently happy to waive the right to receive and make written submissions. This is particularly the case in respect of legislation referred to Senate Committees.

Paragraph (6), which concerns a witness's access to his or her own documents, is virtually never necessary, because it is the policy of most committees to release publicly submissions and associated documents as soon as practicable after their receipt. Nonetheless, it is another declaration of the Senate's intent to preserve the rights of witnesses.

A fourth provision of this nature is contained in paragraph (17), which stipulates that a witness may be given reasonable opportunity to correct the *Hansard* transcript of evidence, and to produce supplementary material. This is both a courtesy and a practical provision and needs no further comment.

Rights of individuals

The remaining paragraphs of the resolution concentrate on the rights of both witnesses and other persons who may be affected by a committee's inquiry. Paragraph (7) covers, at least in part, the topic heading concerning rights of witnesses to refuse to answer a committee's questions on grounds of self-incrimination. A witness can seek to give evidence in private, and self-incrimination would most likely be accepted by a committee as a valid reason for a witness to wish to do so. The committee is required specifically to draw that right to the witness's attention and paragraph (8) insists that the committee warn any such witness that the committee itself, or the Senate, may insist on its publication. Even though the committees are properly required to give such warnings, on the whole, evidence given in private session has rarely been released, much less released improperly.

It is noteworthy, too, that under the Parliamentary Privileges Act 1987, any improper divulging, whether by the witness, by a member or the staff of a committee, or by any other person, of evidence taken in camera may be prosecuted as a criminal offence, as well as its being able to be treated as a contempt under the Senate's normal contempt powers.

Self-incrimination

The direct question of possible self-incrimination is covered by paragraph (10) of the resolution, which provides several levels of protection to a witness. I should emphasise, as I have throughout, that it is only in extreme circumstances that the witness would ever need to invoke the protections contained in this paragraph. Briefly, the witness may raise the question of self-incrimination and the committee may decide immediately not to pursue the question. If it wishes to consider the matter further, the committee must determine *in private* whether it will insist on an answer and must give the witness reasons for the committee's determination. If the committee does so insist, it must pursue the question in private session unless it deems it essential that the question must be answered in public. If the witness still declines to answer the question, the committee itself can take no action against the witness, but may report the facts to the Senate. In the recent history of the Senate, I am not aware of any witness before a committee being pursued to the level of reporting to the Senate.

Relevance

A witness may also under paragraph (10) object to the relevance of committee questions. This matter is also the responsibility of the chairman of the committee, under the immediately preceding paragraph. The combination of the chairman's initiative – with, naturally, an opportunity for committee members to dissent – and a witness's right similarly to query relevance, so that a committee is consciously required to make a determination to pursue the matter, gives the added protection to all persons appearing before committees of ensuring that proceedings are properly conducted and that committees do not canvass matters inappropriate to their terms of reference.

Adverse references

The next three paragraphs of the resolution are designed to ensure that not merely is a witness protected from improper proceedings, but that other persons who might come within the purview of committees, and may be adversely or improperly reflected upon under the protection of parliamentary privilege, have their rights also taken into account. Unfortunately, given the nature of certain inquiries, it is inevitable and unavoidable that persons can be named adversely, whether justly or unjustly.

The protections accorded to such persons are as follows:

The committee may realise from written submissions that public evidence will reflect adversely on a person; under paragraph (11), it might choose to receive such evidence, including the written submission, in private with the intention of either retaining the evidence as in camera evidence or not permitting its release until the person has had an opportunity to respond. It may also release a 'sanitised' version of the evidence or, if it considers a submission irrelevant to its proceedings, will return it to the submittor.

Sometimes, however, an adverse comment may be made unexpectedly at a public hearing. If the adverse material is not relevant to the committee's inquiry, the committee is empowered under paragraph (12) to expunge the *Hansard* record and forbid the publication of the evidence. However, I do not regard this generally as either an effective or a desirable way of proceeding. For example, with most committee proceedings televised throughout Parliament House, it is virtually impossible to prevent such publication. In any case, it may cause the mischief that non-publication is designed to prevent, that is, giving prominence to a matter which might otherwise not be noted by a less-than-attentive media.

So far as I am concerned, if adverse evidence is absolutely imperative to enable a committee to conduct an effective inquiry – and I have been on several committees where this has certainly been the case – the greatest protection that a committee can provide is contained in paragraph (13), which enables a person adversely affected by other evidence to respond in the same forum by both written and oral submission, in combination with paragraph (11).

In extreme circumstances, a witness such as a person adversely affected by committee proceedings may wish to be accompanied by counsel, and be given reasonable opportunity to consult counsel during the committee's hearings (paragraphs (14) and (15)). Again, these protections are rarely used.

Public service witnesses

In recognition of the special duties and obligations of public servants to assist Parliamentary Committees, the resolution provides in paragraph (16) that no committee is permitted to ask a public service officer, whether federal, state or territory, to give opinions on matters of policy. Because the line between policy and administration is, in fact, very blurred, there is a further built-in protection which requires committees to give a reasonable opportunity to any such officer to refer questions to superior officers or to a minister. I shall expand on this further in discussion of ministers as witnesses.

Contempt provision

The all-encompassing last paragraph of the resolution is both protective and punitive. This reminds all witnesses that if they are improperly influenced, or threatened or punished, because they have given evidence before committees, the committees are obliged to protect them by reporting to the Senate.

PRIVILEGE RESOLUTION 2

This inevitably leads to a reference of any such matter to the Committee of Privileges which regards its highest duty as the protection of witnesses before other committees and thus the integrity of the proceedings of those committees and the Senate as well. I do not intend to discuss the detailed but slightly different provisions of the Committee of Privileges proceedings, other than to draw attention, given the terms of reference of the seminar, to two provisions which, like all paragraphs of the resolution, override Resolution 1 to the extent of any inconsistencies. These two features are that:

(a) a witness is not required to answer in public any question where the committee has reason to believe that the answer may incriminate the witness (paragraph (5)).

 As previously indicated, other committees may insist that even self-incriminating evidence be given in public;

(b) witnesses are required to be sworn (paragraph (6)).

 Only rarely do other Senate committees swear witnesses.

These and other protections provided by this resolution are at a higher level than those provided under Resolution 1 for the obvious reason that, even though the committee conducts its proceedings as nearly as possible in accordance with normal, inquisitorial, Parliamentary Committee proceedings, its quasi-judicial role demands that it be bound to the greatest possible extent by natural justice provisions. In common with all other committees, however, the committee is an agent of the Senate and thus can only report its findings and recommendations to its parent body.

SUMMARY OF RIGHTS AND OBLIGATIONS OF WITNESSES

The rights and obligations of witnesses before Senate committees, and before joint committees of the Senate and the House of Representatives which are bound by the Senate Standing and other Orders, and the powers of these committees may be summarised as follows:

All Senate and joint committees of inquiry have power to summon witnesses and require the production of documents and to examine witnesses under oath. However, given the co-operative and information-gathering nature of committee inquiries, those powers are rarely exercised.

No committee has the right to impose sanctions on a witness for refusing to appear before the committee or for giving false evidence, whether under oath or otherwise. As delegates of the Senate, such committees can merely report any offence to the Senate. It is the Senate's invariable practice to refer any such matters to the Committee of Privileges for comprehensive examination and report, although there is nothing to prevent the Senate exercising its powers without that advice. Since the passage of the Parliamentary Privileges Act 1987 and the Privilege Resolutions of 1988, the Committee has reported on 29 substantive privilege matters, most of which have derived from other committee proceedings and several of which have involved the protection of witnesses before other committees.

As indicated above, there are special protections available to public servants appearing before Senate and joint committees. It is the committees' normal practice to take evidence directly from the Senate minister in charge of legislation, whether in his or her own capacity or representing ministers from the House of Representatives. Only Senate ministers appear before committees when estimates are examined.

House of Representatives ministers, and indeed other members of the House, are not precluded from appearing before other Senate committees, although it is not customary for them to do so. Parliamentary secretaries, who are members of the Federal Executive Council but do not hold a ministerial post, are not permitted to appear before committees examining estimates, but may do so in other inquiries.

So far as the responsibility of Senate ministers is concerned, they are normally under the same obligation as other witnesses to answer questions fully and truthfully, and are subject to the Senate's contempt powers. However, it is generally accepted that neither the Senate nor its committees can compel a minister or member from the House of Representatives, or from any state or territory legislature, to attend its hearings, although it can seek the permission of the relevant House for any such member or minister to do so, and welcomes voluntary attendance at its hearings.

SPECIFIC POINTS

I now turn to the specific points raised in the letter of invitation for this study group.

Power to call for 'persons, papers and records and to examine witnesses under oath'

Parliamentary Committees must have the unqualified power to summon witnesses and to require the production of documents. Without that power, they cease to be committees of inquiry and become simply study circles, inferior to the various executive-appointed bodies, such as commissions of inquiry, which have the power to compel evidence. The power is indispensable not only for coercing the occasional recalcitrant witness, but in persuading those who are reluctant to appear and who may not give evidence at all if they know it is purely voluntary. The power, however, must be a reserve power, kept in the locker for use only in the most serious cases. Before using the power, a committee should be sure that its exercise is justified by the circumstances and be willing to pursue the matter to the end if a summons is defied. A committee should also be sure that it will be supported by its House in enforcing its summons.

In relation to swearing witnesses, it is normally not necessary or appropriate. It is well established that parliamentary witnesses are obliged to tell the truth whether or not they are sworn.

Procedures if a witness refuses to appear before a committee

As I have indicated, a committee should not issue a summons unless it is willing to pursue the matter to the end and is sure of support of its House. Obviously fine judgment is required, and a committee should be in this situation only in matters of the utmost gravity. Committees should normally arrange matters so that they do not get into that position. In the Australian Senate, as in most parliamentary assemblies, a committee has no power to punish a recalcitrant witness. It can only refer the matter to the whole Senate for judgment. This is an appropriate arrangement, as it allows the witness, in effect, to appeal to the Senate against a committee, and avoids the injustice of a committee being the judge of its own cause. It also avoids the appearance of personal vendettas by committees against particular witnesses.

Power of the committee to punish witnesses who give false evidence under oath or refuse to appear before the committee

As I have said, the power to actually punish a witness does not belong to a committee but to the whole Senate. The ability to impose penalties must, like the ability to issue summons, be a reserve power, to be used only in the most serious cases. Proven cases of deliberately false evidence should properly attract severe penalties. Refusal to appear is an area where there may be mitigating circumstances. The important point is that a tradition must be established that all evidence to Parliament must be honest and accurate even if it is not given under oath.

What are the rights of the witness to refuse to answer the committee's questions for fear of forfeiting his/her own right to a possible fair trial at a later time?

The law of parliamentary privilege means that self-incrimination is technically not an issue in parliamentary inquiries, because a person's parliamentary evidence cannot be used against them in subsequent legal proceedings. Parliamentary witnesses, however, can incriminate themselves in a wider sense, by exposing themselves to public obloquy or giving law enforcement agencies clues as to investigations which might be directed against them. It is best that Parliamentary Committees do not get into the situation of investigating matters which may be the subject of criminal charges, but where this is unavoidable there are procedures, such as hearing evidence in camera, which can be employed. In the Australian Senate, there are procedures for witnesses to object to answering questions on any grounds, including self-incrimination, and committees are obliged to consider and carefully determine their responses to such objections. At the end of the day, a committee can insist on answers.

Role of pressure groups – do the committees hear the general public or the vocal minority?

Pressure groups are an inevitable part of modern politics. They are highly sophisticated and often international in scope. They are usually also very adept at gaining access to the political system and at competently presenting their particular case. As such, they are also in most instances quite recognisable. On the limited occasions where an *ad hoc* group does form over a particular issue, they would already have lobbied parliamentarians and the media and so again would be identifiable. The point, therefore, is that on the whole the vocal minority, while having a valid right to express their particular view, are identifiable, and the view they are expressing usually well recognised.

Additionally, few committee inquiries develop in isolation. They normally have been preceded by a degree of community or government discussion or disquiet and these discussions and or complaints are seldom conducted in private so a body of superficial knowledge is normally available.

Obviously greater vigilance is required where the matter under scrutiny is of a more technical or complex nature with the consequent field of potential witnesses being considerably smaller.

Committees can where possible ensure they receive the views of the community rather than the vocal minority by diligently conducting the various stages of a review; advertising the inquiry; deciding which of the persons or groups who make submissions are called as witnesses; during the actual public hearings; and when weighing and assessing the body of information provided when formulating the report phase.

Where there is concern regarding the perceived narrowness of the views received, committees are capable and should exercise their judgment in carefully seeking out a broader field of view.

The proper conduct of each to these stages should obviate being seen to be the captives of particular pressure groups for this should ensure the committee is cognisant of and takes evidence from a wide diversity of groups.

Most importantly, committees must also be sufficiently well informed and politically alert to be able to test the validity of the claims of pressure groups. Reports and recommendations must be carefully weighed so as to reflect the public evidence. If committees are overwhelmed by pressure groups it is a sign that they do not possess those qualities or that they are in a field inappropriate to parliamentary inquiry.

Are ministers called as witnesses or should the deputy ministers be called? Who is responsible?

It is entirely appropriate that ministers should appear before Parliamentary Committees to explain government policies, actions and legislative proposals. Ministers regularly appear before committees of the Australian Senate. This is in accordance with the principle of ministerial accountability. Committee hearings are far more effective as an instrument of accountability than proceedings in the whole House, such as question time. As a matter of comity between Houses in a bicameral system, a House should not attempt to summon a minister unless that minister is a member of that House and serious circumstances warrant that course. Competent ministers will welcome the opportunity to demonstrate their capacity in the forum of Parliamentary Committees.

CONCLUSION

As I stated at the commencement of this chapter, the Senate and its committees regard voluntary provision of information by all manner of persons and organizations as an important resource. In the main, Senate committee proceedings are sufficiently informal as to ensure a relaxed exchange of information from and between most Senators and witnesses, and it appears that as a general rule witnesses enjoy the experience and appreciate the opportunity to put their views forward.

In the quarter-century and more since the development of the Senate committee system, committees and their staff have become skilled in winnowing the information they require from the submissions and evidence put before them. It is the duty of the committees to ensure that they are not unduly influenced by any lobby group or vocal minority, whether from the public service or interest groups. They, therefore, cast their net wide, on the clear understanding that they will then perform the duty of protecting the information-givers from any retribution as a result of their appearance before committees. It is for these reasons that the Senate and its committees have both adopted and welcomed the resolutions which are the subject of this chapter.

PARLIAMENTARY PRIVILEGE RESOLUTION NO 1 AGREED TO BY THE SENATE ON 25 FEBRUARY 1988

PROCEDURES TO BE OBSERVED BY SENATE COMMITTEES FOR THE PROTECTION OF WITNESSES

That, in their dealings with witnesses, all committees of the Senate shall observe the following procedures:

(1) A witness shall be invited to attend a committee meeting to give evidence. A witness shall be summoned to appear (whether or not the witness was previously invited to appear) only where the committee has made a decision that the circumstances warrant the issue of a summons.

(2) Where a committee desires that a witness produce documents relevant to the committee's inquiry, the witness shall be invited to do so, and an order that documents be produced shall be made (whether or not an invitation to produce documents has previously been made) only where the committee has made a decision that the circumstances warrant such an order.

(3) A witness shall be given reasonable notice of a meeting at which the witness is to appear, and shall be supplied with a copy of the committee's order of reference, a statement of the matters expected to be dealt with during the witness's appearance, and a copy of these procedures. Where appropriate a witness shall be supplied with a transcript of relevant evidence already taken.

(4) A witness shall be given opportunity to make a submission in writing before appearing to give oral evidence.

(5) Where appropriate, reasonable opportunity shall be given for a witness to raise any matters of concern to the witness relating to the witness's submission or the evidence the witness is to give before the witness appears at a meeting.

(6) A witness shall be given reasonable access to any documents that the witness has produced to a committee.

(7) A witness shall be offered, before giving evidence, the opportunity to make application, before or during the hearing of the witness's evidence, for any or all of the witness's evidence to be heard in private session, and shall be invited to give reasons for any such application. If the application is not granted, the witness shall be notified of reasons for that decision.

(8) Before giving any evidence in private session a witness shall be informed whether it is the intention of the committee to publish or present to the Senate all or part of that evidence that it is within the power of the committee to do so, and that the Senate has the authority to order the production and publication of undisclosed evidence.

(9) A chairman of a committee shall take care to ensure that all questions put to witnesses are relevant to the committee's inquiry and that the information sought by those questions is necessary for the purpose of that inquiry. Where a member of a committee requests discussion of a ruling of the chairman on this matter, the committee shall deliberate in private session and determine whether any question which is the subject of the ruling is to be permitted.

(10) Where a witness objects to answering any question put to the witness on any ground, including the ground that the question is not relevant or that the answer may incriminate the witness, the witness shall be invited to state the ground upon which objection to answering the question is taken. Unless the committee determines immediately that the question should not be pressed, the committee shall then consider in private session whether it will insist upon an answer to the question, having regard to the relevance of the question to the committee's inquiry and the importance to the inquiry of the information sought by the question. If the committee determines that it requires an answer to the question, the witness shall be informed of that determination and the reasons for the determination, and shall be required to answer the question only in private session unless the committee determines that it is essential to the committee's inquiry to that question be answered in public session. Where a witness declines to answer a question to which a committee has required an answer, the committee shall report the facts to the Senate.

(11) Where a committee has reason to believe that evidence about to be given may reflect adversely on a person, the committee shall give consideration to hearing that evidence in private session.

(12) Where a witness gives evidence reflecting adversely on a person and the committee is not satisfied that that evidence is relevant to the committee's inquiry, the committee shall give consideration to expunging that evidence from the transcript of evidence, and to forbidding the publication of that evidence.

(13) Where evidence is given which reflects adversely on a person and action of the kind referred to in paragraph (12) is not taken in respect of the evidence, the committee shall provide reasonable opportunity for that person to have access to that evidence and to respond to that evidence by written submission and appearance before the committee.

(14) A witness may make application to be accompanied by counsel and to consult counsel in the course of a meeting at which the witness appears. In considering such an application, a committee shall have regard to the need for the witness to be accompanied by counsel to ensure proper protection of the witness. If an application is not granted, the witness shall be notified of reasons for that decision.

(15) A witness accompanied by counsel shall be given reasonable opportunity to consult counsel during a meeting at which the witness appears.

(16) An officer of a department of the Commonwealth or of a State shall not be asked to give opinions on matters of policy, and shall be given reasonable opportunity to refer questions asked of the officer to superior officers or to a Minister.

(17) Reasonable opportunity shall be afforded to witnesses to make corrections of errors of transcription in the transcript of their evidence and to put before a committee additional material supplementary to their evidence.

(18) Where a committee has any reason to believe that any person has been improperly influenced in respect of evidence which may be given before the committee, or has been subjected to or threatened with any penalty or injury in respect of any evidence given, the committee shall take all reasonable steps to ascertain the facts of the matter. Where the committee considers that the facts disclose that a person may have been improperly influenced or subjected to or threatened with penalty or injury in respect of evidence which may be or has been given before the committee, the committee shall report the facts and its conclusions to the Senate.

SENATE AND JOINT COMMITTEES

STANDING COMMITTEES

- Appropriations and Staffing
- House
- Library
- Privileges
- Procedure
- Publications
- Selection of Bills
- Senators' Interests

LEGISLATIVE SCRUTINY STANDING COMMITTEES

- Regulations and Ordinances
- Scrutiny of Bills

LEGISLATIVE AND GENERAL PURPOSE STANDING COMMITTEES

- Community Affairs Legislation
- Community Affairs References
- Economics Legislation
- Economics References
- Employment, Education and Training Legislation
- Employment, Education and Training References
- Environment, Recreation, Communications and the Arts Legislation
- Environment, Recreation, Communications and the Arts References
- Finance and Public Administration Legislation
- Finance and Public Administration References
- Foreign Affairs, Defence and Trade Legislation

- Foreign Affairs, Defence and Trade References
- Legal and Constitutional Legislation
- Legal and Constitutional References
- Rural and Regional Affairs and Transport Legislation
- Rural and Regional Affairs and Transport References

Select Committees

- Community Standards Relevant to the Supply of Services Utilising Electronic Technologies
- Superannuation
- Uranium Mining and Milling
- Victorian Casino Inquiry

Joint Statutory Committees

- Australian Security Intelligence Organization
- Broadcasting of Parliamentary Proceedings
- Corporations and Securities
- National Crime Authority
- Native Title and the Aboriginal and Torres Strait Islander Land Fund (formerly Native Title)
- Public Accounts
- Public Works

Joint Standing Committees

- Electoral Matters
- Foreign Affairs, Defence and Trade
- Migration
- National Capital and External Territories
- Treaties

SENATE STANDING REFERENCES COMMITTEES – LIST OF CURRENT INQUIRIES

COMMUNITY AFFAIRS REFERENCES COMMITTEE

Current arrangements for the provision of housing assistance in Australia, including the public provision of housing, cash subsidies and taxation measures, and options for reform of those arrangements.

Fairness of the recent settlement offered to human pituitary hormones recipients by the Commonwealth government and whether public safety has been protected in relation to Australian Human Pituitary Hormone Programme.

ECONOMICS REFERENCES COMMITTEE

Promoting Australian Industry: elements of industry policies in Australia.

EMPLOYMENT, EDUCATION AND TRAINING REFERENCES COMMITTEE

The status of teachers and the development of the teaching profession during the next five years.

ENVIRONMENT, RECREATION, COMMUNICATIONS AND THE ARTS REFERENCES COMMITTEE

The management of water and biological nutrients in Australia.

The question of balancing public access with the principle of 'user pays' in order to defray the public costs of maintaining natural and cultural heritage assets such as national parks and museums with particular consideration to issues of fairness and equity.

Powers of the Commonwealth in environmental protection and ecologically sustainable development in Australia.

FINANCE AND PUBLIC ADMINISTRATION REFERENCES COMMITTEE

The necessity for public accountability of all government services provided by government contractors.

CHAPTER 18

THE FUTURE OF THE COMMITTEE SYSTEM

Senator David MacGibbon, Australia

INTRODUCTION

In the United States, the separation of powers between the legislature, the administration and the judiciary has favoured the development of an extensive committee system with considerable powers. However, the Westminster system, with the executive government drawn from the Parliament, has tended to check the proliferation of committees and to inhibit their powers. It is the growing desire for information and accountability from the community and a natural evolution in the parliamentary process over time which has countered the inhibiting tendencies inherent in the Westminster system.

A basis tenet of the Westminster system is that the executive must be accountable to the Parliament. Ministers must accept responsibility for their government's actions by appearing at Question Time and making ministerial statements where appropriate. In practice, since politics is both adversarial and competitive, there are strong pressures on an executive to release as little information as possible to the Parliament.

Party discipline, an inseparable feature of the Westminster system, certainly aids the process of providing the minimum amount of information on occasions, as does the convention that decisions in relation to defence and foreign affairs matters are made by decree of the executive government rather than in legislative form.

The net effect of all of this is that ministers try to conceal information from Parliament. This concealment is not necessarily to cloak mistakes. Rather, it ensures governments are able to maintain as wide a range of options as possible in the unpredictable world of politics.

In the earlier years, the development of committees were actively discouraged by the ministry in the Australian Federal Parliament. That is with the exception of those areas where there would not be competition between the committee and the executive over the course the Parliament might follow.

However, changing public attitudes in all Western democracies have prompted a much better informed and educated electorate to more actively seek information on the actions of their legislators. Consequently, we have seen an increase in Parliamentary Committee activity because a committee system aids significantly in the important process of accountability of the Parliament.

There is another great virtue of the committee system. The problems that beset legislators in national governments are now very complex. All the simple things have been dealt with. Legislative solutions to these complex problems, therefore, are inadequate to varying degrees. No one enters Parliament with a specialised knowledge of all subjects covered by legislation. In fact many enter with no detailed knowledge of any portfolio. Without this detailed knowledge of a specific topic, it is impossible for a member of Parliament to assess the merits of complex legislation.

The executive government's task is made much easier if the members of Parliament are uninformed and they therefore have a vested interest in maintaining this state. The other great benefit, therefore, of the committee system apart from the accountability aspect is that properly handled it provides a means independent of the executive for educating the members of Parliament. Not only can a member be informed on a specific topic but over a period of years a comprehensive knowledge of the whole subject can be obtained if a member has the ability and application to acquire it.

Inextricably linked with the complexity of matters dealt with by the Parliament is the huge and ever growing volume of information required to adequately address issues, which would be impossible to put before the Parliament but which can be sought and sifted through the committee system. Additionally, an increasingly more interactive committee system means experts and interested observers from outside government are able to participate and take a more active role in the decision making process, which is a further positive step in the evolution of the committee system.

In the more than a quarter century that a structured committee system – as opposed to individual committees – has been in use in the Australian Senate, there is little doubt that it has enhanced the Senate's performance of the parliamentary legislative role, particularly its important role in scrutinising the executive.

Let me now turn to the first question.

IS A COMMITTEE SYSTEM NECESSARY OR WITH MODERN TELECOMMUNICATIONS CAN A GOVERNMENT COMMUNICATE WITH THE PUBLIC DIRECTLY?

Yes, emphatically, for the reasons previously outlined, committees are necessary. While governments should engage directly with the public more often, and are certainly providing greater amounts of information today, the fact remains that no effective accountability can be mediated this way.

WILL THE COMMITTEE SYSTEM CONTINUE TO EVOLVE OR IS IT STATIC?

The system will continue to evolve. At present in the Australian Senate, the committee system has been expanded with respect to the number of committees beyond a sustainable level. In short, there are too many committees. A rationalisation process which reduces the number of committees will have to take place in time if only on the grounds that there are not enough senators to go around. There will be fewer Standing Committees. But, those which remain will be structured with terms of reference which allow wider ambits for their operation.

With respect to those committees which have as their role some element of accountability, an audit like process will emerge where the committee has the role to examine any area of a portfolio in great detail rather than attempt an overall oversight of the whole portfolio.

With respect to committees in general, there must be moves to separate out, in so far as it is practicable, party political committees from genuine Parliamentary Committees. The genuine Parliamentary Committees, the Standing Committees which relate to the review of legislation and the oversight of the executive, should be bipartisan and, therefore, objective in their operation. For those matters of controversy or dispute between the political parties in the Parliament, ad hoc or Select Committees as they are called in Australia, but not in the United Kingdom, should be set up to deal with that one issue. They have a finite life and can be as disputative as the members wish. Such a clear clinical division is not always possible in practice but it is a goal to be sought.

The great evolution in committees will inevitably come from modern communications and modern databases. International video conferencing links are currently used in Australian committees as well as telephonic conferencing around the country. The almost instant retrieval of data and the analysis of that data through computer based information systems, not only available to committees but to each member of Parliament in their own office, offers enormous opportunities to committees to extend the range of their deliberations.

IS THE SYSTEM EFFECTIVE AND HOW CAN IT BE IMPROVED?

The system is effective in its present form. In the Australian Parliament, it is the usual practice when a committee conducts an inquiry for the committee to make a number of recommendations. In the Senate, the government must respond in a written report within three months to those recommendations accepting or rejecting them with reasons.

A considerable number of inquiries are initiated because of obvious short-comings in government legislation or policy so it can hardly be expected that a government rushes to embrace and implement the recommendations of a committee.

If a government declines to implement immediately, the recommendations of a committee all has not been in vain. Committees earn reputations for themselves and if a report is well reasoned with a high standard of scholarship then much to the chagrin of the government it becomes a reference text for analysts, educational institutions and most importantly for public servants. The report lives on the shelves long after the government's tacit rejection has been forgotten and thereby influences future policy in many cases.

WHAT IMPROVEMENTS CAN BE MADE?

The members who make up the committees are very important. Whatever the selection process for committee membership, it should strive to select those with an interest in and enthusiasm for the work of the committee and the intellectual resources to cope with the subject. The role of the chairman, while first among equals, is very important, for the knowledge, judgment and leadership of a committee chairman is at a premium.

At the same time, the committee must have adequate resources. This starts with an adequate budget. Most committees operate in a specialised area and there must be at least one adviser to the committee with professional knowledge of the subject. That person must be able to write reports lucidly and in a pleasant, readable style. In all but the smallest of committees, the committee secretariat should consist of at least two members. Budgetary support is also needed for advertising for public inquiries, the travel of the committee, for witnesses to attend public hearings, and for publication of reports.

The committee must be endowed with adequate powers under its terms of reference to perform its task.

Committees must be free from all direction or pressure from the executive government. Subtle pressures can be exerted on committees by the executive attempting to propose references for inquiries by the committee, restraining the appearance of witnesses when they are public servants or by limiting the budget resources of the committee.

Since 1970, when the Senate committee structure was established, all committees involved in the scrutiny of the executive government, particularly proposed expenditure by those governments, have had some difficulty in acquiring information, whether by documentation or through oral evidence.

The committees succeeded in the late 1970s in ensuring the provision of expenditure information in a standardised form, through the production of explanatory notes of departments and agencies.

Since then, however, new obstacles have been put in the path of parliamentary scrutiny. For example, the change to programme budgeting which occurred in the mid-1980s also meant a change in the format of those notes, so that less information is now produced than was available 20 years ago. At present, the Senate Finance and Public Administration Legislation Committee, on behalf of all the other committees, is examining the best possible format of those notes to get back to where we once were.

Furthermore, as government bodies and agencies are part-privatised or metamorphosed into 44 government business enterprises, and as all governments increasingly resort to out-sourcing for the provision of previously publicly delivered services, the lines of accountability are increasingly blurred. Bureaucrats wishing to avoid accountability to Parliament are calling in aid such excuses as 'the information is commercial-in-confidence'. Again, the Finance and Public Administration References Committee is currently examining the necessity for public accountability of all government services provided by government contractors.

These and other changes to public service delivery, and to the structures and ethos of the public service, necessitate the evolution of parliamentary structures generally, and committee structures in particular, to adjust the relationship between the Parliament and the executive. At present, the nature of the public service in Australia is being redefined through the introduction of a new Public Service Bill which completely replaces the heavily amended Public Service Act passed by the Commonwealth Parliament in 1922. This Bill is at present being examined by the Joint Committee of Public Accounts; notwithstanding the thorough examination that that committee will undertake there will be areas which the Senate will determine require further examination by one of its own committees.

The Bill will be complemented by a separate Bill to restructure the parliamentary services, acknowledging legislatively for the first time the separation of powers concept which underpins the written Australian Constitution. Given the far reaching nature of the proposal, and its implications for the Parliament as a whole, again I have little doubt that committees will be called in aid by either or both Houses of the Australian Parliament to ensure that the structural implications for the Parliament and its committees are teased out and understood by parliamentary decision makers.

With the volume and complexity of legislation that comes before the Parliament annually averaging about 200 Bills – with the associated complex explanatory memoranda and the equally complex submissions which are made by the plethora of interest groups which have created themselves to provide alternative sources of information and advice to senators and members, a mechanism to 'package' the information available to all members of Parliament, including ministers, is a requirement of the modern age.

In addition, with the advent of a wide range of computerised databases, and access to the internet by all senators and members, the volume of information potentially available has grown exponentially. A Parliamentary Committee system does, in my view, provide a framework for such packaging.

COMMITTEE SCRUTINY AND EVALUATION OF LEGISLATION

Increasingly, legislation is and must be referred to committees. At present, about one-third of all Bills are referred to Senate Committees. A major problem for the committees is that Bills which have been prepared in secret by governments and their departments, often with advice from selected interest groups, burst on to the public scene with the government expectation of their rapid passage through the Parliament. The single essential role of an effective committee system must be to open up the process. I have a distinct impression that perhaps up to a quarter of the 200 Bills the Australian Parliament passes each year are corrections to hastily prepared, drafted, and thought-through legislation of previous times. Without public input, from a much wider range of resources than those available to – let alone used by – government, legislation will be an imperfect mechanism for implementation of government policy.

The problem for committees is that normally in Australia they are perceived by government as a nuisance, rather than as a resource to be used by government to enhance decision making. Consequently, the pressure has been on committees to examine legislation superficially, and to recommend its passage with minimal or no amendment. This pressure has led in turn to an all-too-frequent division of committee reports on party lines, regardless of the weight of evidence before the committee, with government senators recommending no or cosmetic, changes and non-government senators foreshadowing significant amendments which are not made available until debate occurs in the chamber. Thus, an enormous amount of available chamber time is lost through the requirement to negotiate in the chamber what should more appropriately have been sorted out during committee proceedings. This is a pity, because if time is given to receive and evaluate evidence, and to negotiate a more desirable legislative outcome, the delivery of agreed policy objectives is likely to be smoother than that which results from a continuation of entrenched positions.

This problem also exists even where there is an acceptance by government and non-government senators that changes of substance are needed. A committee report, and the associated evidence and submissions, may declare that substantial amendments are required.

Instead of these amendments being prepared for committee consideration, the committee reports to the chamber and again precious chamber time is used to negotiate through some hundreds of substantial amendments which could more appropriately be dealt with by a smaller, delegated and specialised body, the members of which have developed expertise in dealing with a particular subject matter.

USE OF TECHNOLOGY

If proposed amendments arising out of committee hearings were referred back to committees, the procedure could be refined through the optimal used of already-existing technology to enable committee members, ministers and their public service advisers, and interested bodies to evaluate proposed changes. At present, all amendments are prepared for circulation as separate entities in the chamber, and there is no attempt made to incorporate them in a Bill, much less a principal act, before passage through the chamber. Technological capacity to insert amendments in text and disseminate the revised text by means such as the internet would ensure the widest possible public input before legislative proposals were entrenched in law.

All committees may meet 'electronically', without members being physically present in one place, and for some considerable time have taken evidence by satellite and by video conference. In a vast country such as Australia, these new means of communication must be incorporated into regular committee procedures, to enhance the capacity of committees to perform their already-extensive role of communicating directly with the people.

In fact, the use of modern telecommunications and other advanced technologies does not make committees redundant, as implied by this agenda item. The capacity of government to communicate with the people, by whatever means, has never been its strong point, and all the new technology in the world is not likely to change that. So long as there is a culture of secrecy in government circles, the need for a Parliamentary Committee structure, enhanced by new technology, is likely to be greater. It follows, therefore, that any good Parliamentary Committee structure will continue to evolve to meet new requirements, and will neither be static nor rest on its hard-won laurels if it is determined to take its place in modern society.

WHAT IS THE FUTURE OF THE COMMITTEE SYSTEM AND WILL IT FOLLOW THE AMERICAN PATTERN?

There is no way the progress made by committees can be withdrawn. Committees in the Westminster system will become more intrusive on the government and take more power unto themselves – with the approval of the chamber. In that sense, our committees will be starting down the congressional path.

To some extent, we are down that path already. The televising of Senate committee hearings has induced lapses of wildly histrionic behaviour in front of the cameras in several senators and at least one witness to date. This is an undesirable move for the deliberations of the committee but probably nothing can be done about it.

It is also possible to envisage, though it is unlikely, that, if a committee was thwarted in its endeavours and a majority of senators supported it, the Senate could resolve not to fund the particular programme in which the dispute occurred. This is drawing a long bow admittedly in the Australian system but the situation may well arise in the years ahead.

So what is the future of the Australian Senate committee system?

I envisage it as continuing to develop as one of the few alternatives to governmental hegemony.

The two most important constraints on committees are the time resource of members themselves and the funding they require for effective operation. For example, in realistic terms, of the 37 government senators only about 25 are available for service on Parliamentary Committees.

As outlined above how far congressional features permeate the system is difficult to determine. Already, like the US congressional committees, Senate committees are semi-autonomous and have enormous *de facto* powers. Unlike congressional committees, Senate committees are not overwhelmed and driven by their staff. There is no concept of majority and minority staffers. Senate staff serve all the committee members equally. Nor is there any practice for staff to set the agenda, or substitute for committee members. Decision making at committee level rests with the members, led by their first among equals, the chairman. Nor do committees initiate legislation: they normally evaluate government legislative proposals. However, like congressional committees, they are firmly committed to scrutinising the activities of government and have a commitment to expose executive practices through the light of publicity.

CONCLUSION

Any committee system is always open to improvement and, in a dynamic institution, changes are constant, usually subtle, sometimes dramatic, but always occurring. If we do not succeed in adapting, there will be no future for any Parliamentary Committee system. It is, therefore, for us to exert our determination as parliamentarians to ensure the survival of this most basic tool of legislatures.

CHAPTER 19

SERVICES, STAFF AND FACILITIES PROVIDED TO COMMITTEES OF THE CANADIAN HOUSE OF COMMONS

Peter Milliken, MP, Canada

INTRODUCTION

This chapter provides general information on the services, staff and facilities available to committees of the House of Commons in the federal Parliament of Canada. It does not, however, include a discussion of the services, staff and facilities available to the committees of the Senate of Canada or to the committees of each of the 12 provincial and territorial legislatures.[1]

POWERS

Committees are empowered to examine and inquire into all such matters as may be referred to them by the House of Commons. They can also study and report on all matters relating to the mandate, management and operation of the department or departments of government that are assigned to them.

Committees have the ability to invite or summon witnesses and examine these individuals under oath. Witnesses can be reimbursed for their reasonable travelling and living expenses.

Each committee prepares and submits an annual budget to the Liaison Committee of the House of Commons for approval. The Liaison Committee is composed of the chairs of all the Standing Committees of the House. The various costs and expenses that the committee may incur are charged against this budget.

---

1 This document is based on the Committees Directorate publications entitled *Operations Manual* and *Committees of the House of Commons: A Practical Guide,* along with input from staff of the House of Commons Committees Directorate. The information contained in this chapter is current as of 10 July 1997.

SERVICES

Translation

During a meeting of a House of Commons, committee members are provided with translation services for the proceedings. Translation of meetings is usually simultaneous but can also be consecutive, where the individual speaks and then everyone waits for the translator to translate before proceeding. Escort translation is also available, where the translator speaks directly to the person requiring translation services. Consecutive translation and escort translation are rarely used services.

Broadcasting

Committee meetings may be broadcast on the Canadian Parliamentary Channel (CPaC) and over the OASIS network, if the facilities exist in the meeting room. The audio portions of public committee meetings are broadcast over the OASIS network, if the meeting room is equipped for this feature (as are most committee rooms on Parliament Hill). The OASIS network is a local audio and video network that can be accessed by those individuals located on the parliamentary precinct. The Press has full access to this network and can retransmit the proceedings or use it for other purposes.

Video transmission of committees meetings can be also be made over the OASIS network (if the meeting room is equipped for this feature). These transmissions can then be re-broadcast on the Canadian Parliamentary Channel, a cable television channel available to most Canadian cable subscribers.

Audio-visual equipment

The House of Commons can provide committees with any audio-visual equipment they may need to carry out a meeting. This can include, but is not necessarily restricted to, audio playback equipment, videotape machines and monitors, and large screen projector systems.

Refreshments

Committees can choose to purchase coffee and other beverages for any meeting. These catering services are provided by the Parliamentary Restaurant Services.

Messengers

All committees share one messenger to hand deliver documents within the parliamentary precinct. Each committee, while a meeting is in progress, is provided with a receptionist to assist with telephone calls, summon messengers and other duties at a meeting.

Security services

Buildings on the parliamentary precinct are provided with security at the entrances by the Security Services of the House of Commons and of the Senate. If the Chair believes that the committee members or its witnesses are in need of additional security services, the committee can request that a security guard be posted at the entrance to the meeting and, if necessary, assigned to escort a witness. Committee clerks are provided with a 'panic button'. This small electronic device can be used to summon security services to a committee meeting in an emergency.

Committee documents

The services of the Committee Reporting Service are used to record, transcribe and edit the verbatim transcripts of the proceedings. These transcripts are translated and then made available on the internet.

Committee members can request to be provided with a copy of the unedited transcripts of meetings. When the transcripts of meetings are fully translated and edited, they are made available to all members, and to the public, on the internet. The *Minutes of Proceedings* of the committee are also available, upon request. Committee members are also provided with briefing notes in both official languages for most meetings, prepared by the Parliamentary Research Branch.

Committee members are provided with a copy of all briefs submitted to the committee in both official languages. If this is not possible, the briefs are given to the members of the committee in the original language of the document with an accompanying executive summary in the other official language. Committees usually adopt a motion at the beginning of each session of Parliament regarding the translation of documents.

All documents published by the committee are in both official languages.

Internet space

The Parliament of Canada has an extensive internet web site at http://www.parl.gc.ca. Committees are able to use space on the Parliamentary internet site to call for witnesses, advertise, or place documents for the public to view.

The section of the Parliamentary internet site devoted to House of Commons committees contains a general description of the types, roles and operations of committees. This is in addition to having committee documents placed on the internet at the same location. The following committee documents can presently be found on the internet:

- evidence of the committee;
- Minutes of Proceedings of the committee;
- notices of upcoming meetings;
- selected reports;
- membership of the committee.

Advertising

Committees can advertise on the Canadian Parliamentary Channel, free of charge. If the committee wishes to pay the necessary costs, it can also advertise with any other media organizations, such as newspapers, commercial television or radio.

Travel

Committees can travel within and outside of Canada to hear witnesses and/or to observe activities. This travel by the committee can be in any form including by train, bus or air, but the committee is required to pay all associated costs. Air travel can be either by commercial airlines or private air charters.

Accommodation for members and staff of the committee can also be provided while they are travelling on committee business, but the committee must pay the costs associated with this.

To assist members and staff with the expenses associated with the purchase of meals and other services while travelling on committee business, they are provided with an allowance. Members of the committee are provided with the members *Per Diem* Allowance, a non-accountable *per diem.* Staff is provided with the Staff *Per Diem* Allowance, which is an accountable *per diem.*

Media relations

If the members of a committee are engaged in a study whose subject matter necessitates the hiring of a media relations consultant or firm, the committee is empowered to do this. The committee will pay for costs for these services.

From time to time, it is necessary for the committee to hold press conferences. The National Press Theatre, located across the street from the Parliament Buildings, and Room 130-S in the Centre Block of the Parliament Buildings, are both press conference facilities that are available, upon request, should they be needed. To assist in communicating with the media, committees can prepare and distribute press releases and press kits. If the committee wishes, they can arrange to provide journalists with a 'lock up' prior to its release. A 'lock up' involves providing journalists with access to a room on the day that the committee will be tabling a complex or technical report in Parliament. This gives journalists a chance to review the documents in question immediately prior to their release so that they are better able to report on them when they are tabled in the House of Commons. These journalists may not reveal the contents of these documents until they have been presented in Parliament.

Mail

The House of Commons provides committees with access to its internal mail system. This system allows committees to deliver and receive mail and parliamentary publications. It should be noted that the principal clerk of the Committees Directorate has 'franking' privileges, which permits committees to mail items free of charge within Canada.

COMMITTEE STAFF

Each committee is assisted by a clerk, a research team and, where necessary, procedural clerks, legal counsel and outside consultants.

Committee clerk

The clerk of the committee is the principal adviser to both the chair and the committee on matters of parliamentary procedure. Should a question of procedure arise during a meeting, the chair or the members may consult the clerk. As a non-partisan and independent officer of the committee, the clerk serves all members of the committee and representatives of all parties equally.

During the committee's study of legislation, the clerk will prepare a list containing the members' proposed amendments in their appropriate order and advises the chair on the receivability of each amendment.

In addition to the role as procedural adviser, the clerk is also the committee's administrator. This is fundamental in assisting the committee to function: the clerk is the coordinator, organizer and liaison officer for the committee and performs a wide variety of administrative tasks. These tasks include the following:

- preparation for public meetings related to the committee's study or consideration of a Bill;
- marking arrangements for, and attendance at, meetings of the committee and its subcommittees;
- preparation and certification of the Minutes of Proceedings (The clerk must also ensure the printing of the *Minutes of Proceedings and Evidence* and reports to the House);
- drafting and sending the Notices of Meetings through the electronic mail system, reservation of meeting rooms, and supervision of the work of the required support staff;
- responsibility for the committee's correspondence, arrangements for witnesses and reimbursement of approved witness expenses;
- co-ordination of the translation and distribution of all committee documents and briefs to the Members;
- co-ordination of the production of all reports to the House and, in the case of Bills, drafting of the report;
- supervision of all logistical and other operations when the committee travels, including all of the accompanying support staff;
- advising the Chair on consultants' contracts;
- preparation of the committee budget and processing of all committee expenses with such financial authority as may be delegated by the Chair.

The clerk must also act as the liaison officer with several other branches and services of the House of Commons, including the Table Research Branch and legislative counsel. This allows the committee to consult with experts in the Table Research Branch, who advise on procedural on matters, and with legislative counsel, which provide support during clause by clause study of a Bill as well as assisting Members in drafting amendments.

Researchers from the Library of Parliament

The Parliamentary Research Branch of the Library of Parliament is staffed by researchers in various disciplines, who are available to each committee. The work undertaken, which varies according to the needs of the committee, may include:

- assistance in drawing up a plan of action and schedule for committee hearings;
- preparing a proposed list of witnesses to be heard by the committee;
- preparing briefing notes and background documents on issues involved in the committee's order of reference and/or in preparation of public hearings (summaries of briefs, suggested lines of questioning);
- the preparation of in-depth research papers on specific subjects; and
- drafting committee reports and press releases.

In addition, the Parliamentary Research Branch may be called upon to provide oral briefings to committees on issues being studied, often accompanied by a briefing book, which may include comparative charts and commentaries on issues and the evidence. Such briefing sessions may also relate to discussions of a draft report prior to its release. Researchers also ensure the compilation and analysis of all evidence heard by a committee. In the case of a committee that is responsible for studying a particular piece of legislation, the researchers may also prepare a summary of the Bill.

Consultants

Parliamentary committees charged with a particularly complex subject also have the power to engage experts (lawyers, accountants, economists, etc.) as required to fulfil their research needs. If specialists in a subject area are not available from the Parliamentary Research Branch, the committee, by means of a contract, may hire the necessary consultants. The committee determines the mandate and duration of such contracts.

FACILITIES

There are approximately 13 meeting rooms that the House of Commons committees have access to on the parliamentary precinct. These rooms vary in size, seating capacity, and the type of audio and video broadcasting facilities available. Generally, these meeting rooms provide tables and seating for members, committee staff and limited seating for the public. There are also facilities in each room to enable simultaneous translation of the proceedings.

In addition to these meeting rooms, committees have access to the government facilities at Meech Lake (O'Brian House and Wilson House) for in camera meetings. Those facilities on Parliament Hill designated as Senate committee meeting rooms may also be used by House of Commons committees with the consent of the Senate.

CHAPTER 20

THE FUTURE OF THE COMMITTEE SYSTEM

Peter Milliken, MP, Canada

INTRODUCTION

Committees are an integral part of the modern parliamentary system. A great deal of important work is done by them, and many parliamentarians find that committee work is among the most satisfying and fulfilling part of their jobs. Committees are often more collegial and informal than the House of Commons itself, and the atmosphere is frequently less partisan and adversarial. Witnesses can be called and questioned, and more substantive work undertaken.

In Canada, the role and importance of committees of the House of Commons has increased dramatically over the past 20 or 30 years. Under the Standing Orders, committees have considerable autonomy and powers, and a number of committees have managed to carve out a reputation and persona for themselves. Much of the potential of committees, however, remains unrealized. In addition, there remains some uncertainty and debate over exactly what should be the function or purpose of committees in a parliamentary system.

This chapter will look at the future of the committee system, and discuss some of the issues facing committees. The focus will be on the committee system in the Canadian House of Commons, although references and comparisons will be made to committee systems in the Senate of Canada and in other jurisdictions. There is, of course, always some risk in looking in isolation at one aspect of the legislative process – such as committees – since this ignores the inter-connectedness of the system as a whole. Nevertheless, many of the challenges regarding committees in Canada are also faced by parliamentarians elsewhere in the Commonwealth, so the Canadian experience may be useful and relevant.

The chapter begins with a brief history of the evolution of the committee system in the Canadian House of Commons, and a description of the current regime. It will then discuss a number of areas in which proposals for change have been made or where problems are apparent.

It should be noted at the outset that there was a federal general election in June 1997, as a result of which a new House of Commons was elected. At the beginning of any new Parliament, it is not uncommon for the committee system to be re-assessed and changed. This is particularly likely to happen as a consequence of the new configuration of the House of Commons: the government party – the Liberals – have a very slight majority, while there are four recognized opposition parties, including two with about 20 Members each. The composition of the House always influences the structure of committees, but it is particularly likely to for the next little while. The parties also have varying regional bases, and represent a range of ideological views, and this is also likely to have a major impact on the committee system.

EVOLUTION OF THE CANADIAN COMMITTEE SYSTEM[1]

Although there have been Parliamentary Committees in Canada since the country was established in 1867, originally, they were not an important part of the parliamentary process. Of the original rules adopted by the House, few were directly concerned with Standing or Special (Select) Committees. Until 1906, the Standing Orders did not contain any list of the committees to be set up, nor did they set out their powers, procedures or other matters relating to committees. The relative unimportance of committees was attributable to the fact that there was not a great deal of business before the House – initially, much of it consisted of private legislation – and the House met for fairly short periods of time. There was, however, a nascent system of specialist committees, although some committees that were appointed at the beginning of a session remained moribund.

Even after 1906 when the rules made provision for Standing Committees, their usefulness was limited. Part of this was because of their unwieldy size: a motion in 1925 to reduce the membership of Standing Committees to 'secure more regular attendance and promote efficiency'[2] led to a recommendation that the membership of each committee be *limited* to not more than 30. Changes to the rules regarding committees were made periodically – for instance in 1927 – but were often related to the responsibilities of committees in relation of the business of supply. By 1945, there was no doubt that committees were being used increasingly to study Bills and other subject matters – although the text of the Standing Orders had changed little from

1 More detailed background on the development of the committee system in the Canadian House of Commons can be found in Rush, M, 'The development of the Committee System in the Canadian House of Commons – I Diagnosis and revitalisation' (1974) LV (2) The Parliamentarian, April, pp 86–94; 'II Reassessment and reform' (1974) LV (3) The Parliamentarian, July, pp 149–58; March, RR, 'Parliamentary Committees since 1968', Prepared for the Canadian Political Science Association, 1 June 1971; and Hockin, TA, 'The advance of Standing Committees in Canada's House of Commons' (1970) XIII (2) Canadian Public Administration, Summer, pp 185–202.

2 Canada, House of Commons, *Debates,* 11 March 1925, pp 1034–41.

1906 – and the workload of committees was rising significantly. A few new committees were established over the years, and it is clear from the debates on these amendments that Members felt that committees would play an increasingly prominent role in the functioning of the House. Some committees, such as the Agriculture Committee, performed useful investigations, while the Veterans' Affairs Committee was influential in establishing the scheme of benefits for veterans after the Second World War. One authority concluded: 'But in spite of these and other exceptions, the committees were generally not active, nor were they an important part of Parliament.'[3]

In the late 1950s, the first of many special committees on procedure was established to review the rules of the House. Throughout the 1960s, attempts were made to reorganize the committee structure, and to make related changes. In December 1968, the committee system received its most drastic overhaul since Confederation when the Trudeau government introduced a package of amendments: the size of committees was reduced to 20 members; committees were given the right to sit while the House was sitting and during adjournments, and the right to delegate all their powers, except reporting to the House, to sub-committees; changes in membership were made easier; and, most importantly, there were changes in the functions given to committees: the departmental spending estimates were to be automatically referred to the appropriate committees for review, and government legislation was to be referred to the Standing Committees after second reading. As Professor CES Franks has commented:

> The Canadian House of Commons now had not only its comprehensive system of specialist committees covering the programmes of government, but a new assignment of responsibilities which ensured that they would meet frequently and occupy much of the time and energy of members of Parliament.[4]

According to one study:

> While the text of the Standing Orders changed little from 1867 to 1965 and from 1968 to 1982, the practices and procedures governing the conduct of meetings of both Standing and Special Committees, the duties and responsibilities of the Chairmen and the manner of proceeding in the study of estimates and the legislation referred to them were in a constant state of evolution.[5]

The early 1980s were a period when the procedures generally of the House of Commons came under scrutiny and review, and many important changes were proposed. These culminated in the appointment of the Special

3 Franks, CES, *The Parliament of Canada, 1987*, Toronto: Toronto UP, p 162.

4 *Ibid*, p 163.

5 Canada, House of Commons, *Annotated Standing Orders*, 1989, pp 346–47.

Committee on Reform of the House of Commons (the McGrath Committee), which was appointed in 1984 at the beginning of the 33rd Parliament. One of the Committee's prime objectives was to enhance the role of Private Members, and the Standing Committee system was an important tool in this regard. The Committee's recommendations led to a restructuring of the committee system basically to reflect the organization of government. It also recommended smaller committees – ideally, seven members – and a prohibition on parliamentary secretaries from sitting on committees so as to enhance their independence. The McGrath Committee also advocated the establishment of Legislative Committees to consider Bills after second reading, rather than referring them to Standing Committees, and the review of certain order in council appointments by the Standing Committees.

Most importantly, the committee recommended that committees be given the power to study any matter within their mandates without the requirement of an order of reference from the House of Commons. For the first time, committees would be able to decide what issues they wished to examine and how to organize their work. These and other recommendations of the committee were, for the most part, implemented in the mid-1980s. The result was a much higher profile for Parliamentary Committees and, on occasion, conflicts between committees and ministers.

Various changes have been made since 1990. The number of committees has been reduced somewhat. The size of Standing Committees has also increased, partly in order to reflect the party standings in the House. After several years of experience with Legislative Committees, they have fallen into disuse, and Bills are now referred to Standing Committees for study. Parliamentary secretaries are once again allowed to sit on Standing Committees. Limited broadcasting of committee proceedings was introduced.

The committee system of the Canadian House of Commons has improved dramatically over the past 15 or 20 years. It is a vital part of the parliamentary process, and one that has enjoyed considerable success. While much productive work is carried out in committees, and many members find that their most satisfying work is done there, there remain areas of dissatisfaction. Committees still do not fully satisfy the expectations of the public nor the ambitions of MPs. Despite procedural reforms, many of the same problems remain today that existed in the past.

In 1993, the Liaison Committee of the House of Commons – whose membership consists of the chairs of the different Standing Committees – reviewed committee effectiveness, and concluded that:

> ... while the opportunity for committees to offer advice on policy has been substantially increased, results measured by the influence that committees have had on the actions of the government or by their success in generating public debate have been mixed. The potential of some committees is not being

> realized because committees are not being accorded the importance that they should have in an effective Parliament.[6]

The committee put forward several explanations for the gap between perceived powers and actual improvements, including: structural deficiencies in the way committees are organized; attempts to achieve objectives that may not be attainable in the Canadian parliamentary system; lack of experience on the part of members as to how to maximize the new potential of committees; lack of public awareness of what committees are doing and of public input into their work; the work of committees is too often not taken seriously by ministers and public servants; and Parliament itself does not accord adequate importance to the work of its committees.

Proposals have been made over the years as to how the committee system could be improved. Before proceeding to a consideration of these, however, it might be worthwhile to look at the more basic question of what are the role and function of committees in a parliamentary system.

THE ROLE OF PARLIAMENTARY COMMITTEES

One of the difficulties in assessing the success of Parliamentary Committees or how they should evolve in the future is the uncertainty or confusion over exactly what their role is.

This problem is particularly acute in Canada, where the influence of the United States is strong. As Professor Franks has noted, Canadians have the inescapable example of US congressional committees which are active, highly visible, and give elected senators and representatives a strong voice in the management of the nation's affairs.[7] The 1993 Report of the Liaison Committee on Committee Effectiveness also noted this influence:

> Proximity to the United States is a major reason for the grander aspirations of Canadian Parliamentary Committees. The interest Canadians take in the US political scene generates expectations that simply cannot be realized under the Canadian political system. Many Canadians, including members of Parliament, tend to have American committees in mind when they measure the achievements of Canadian committees, ignoring the substantial differences in the two political systems.[8]

---

6 Liaison Committee, Canada, House of Commons, Report on Committee Effectiveness, 1993, re-printed in *Parliamentary Government,* Number 43 (June 1993), p 3.

7 *Op cit,* Franks, fn 3, p 161.

8 *Op cit,* Liaison Committee, fn 6, p 13.

'The dilemma in Canada', according to the Liaison Committee, 'is that the political culture expects Parliamentary Committees to behave like US committees and to be as influential.[9] This can lead to unrealistic expectations, and comparisons of apples and oranges.

As the Liaison Committee and other commentators have pointed out, it is necessary to examine the rationale of a committee system. It is useful periodically to re-think the fundamentals underlying committees.

In his 1955 classic work, *Government by Committee*, KC Wheare observed that there are six basic roles of Parliamentary Committees: to advise; to inquire; to administer; to legislate; to negotiate; and to scrutinize and control.[10] Other authors have noted a number of incidental functions of Parliamentary Committees. FA Kunz, for instance, in his study of the Canadian Senate, noted that committees can educate parliamentarians, that they can provide a forum for the articulation of interests and can form a liaison between Parliament and government departments.[11] Professor CES Franks has stated that committees can mobilize consent within the Canadian public and assist in achieving legitimacy for legislative measures. He has also noted that committees provide a point of access to the system of power for interest groups.[12]

Paul Pross noted that committees play a role in Parliament's publicizing capacity.[13] Grace Skogstad has observed that committees can help achieve consensus among competing interests and can perform a representative and conflict management function.[14] Neville Johnson has stated that, through its committees, parliamentarians can learn about administrative structures, and that committees can impact on the way officials conduct business and behave and on the climate of public opinion regarding the problems that they study.[15] Graham White and Gary Levy have argued that committees have the potential for influencing government activity, contribute to the policy process and enhance government accountability.[16]

---

9 *Op cit*, Liaison Committee, fn 6.

10 Wheare, KC, *Government by Committee: An Essay on the British Constitution*, 1965, Oxford: Clarendon.

11 Kunz, FA, *The Modern Senate of Canada*, 1965, Toronto: Toronto UP, p 258.

12 *Op cit*, Franks, fn 3, pp 161–85.

13 Pross, PA, 'Parliamentary influence and the diffusion of power' (1985) Canadian Journal of Political Science, pp 235–66.

14 Skogstad, G, 'Interest groups, representation and conflict management in the Standing Committees of the Canadian House of Commons' (1985) Canadian Journal of Political Science, pp 739–72.

15 Johnson, N, 'Select Committees as tools of parliamentary reform', in Walkland, SA *et al*, *The Commons in the 70s*, 1977, London: Fontana, p 196.

16 White, G and Levy, G, *Provincial and Territorial Legislatures*, 1989, Toronto: Toronto UP, p 4.

At the same time, it is important to remember the parliamentary context and what Parliamentary Committees cannot or should not do. Professor Sharon L Sutherland has written:

> In the context of British-style Cabinet government, the government has no duty – and in fact it has no business – to *share* power with politicians who are not members of the government. Responsible government can only make sense when the government is an identifiable entity within another entity that keeps it responsible.[17]

This echoes a point made by Professor Franks, that 'an argument against strong Parliamentary Committees is that they submerge the distinctions between parties and give power to 'irresponsible' committees rather than a 'responsible' government'.[18] Writing in 1993, Professor Sutherland believed that, with few exceptions, the reformed Standing Committees of the Canadian House of Commons had operated in the role of junior partners to the government 'largely interested in keeping the government out of trouble, and allowed themselves to be used as an agent of discipline against the public service'.[19]

Professor Franks has also pointed out that some of the functions – such as the handling of Bills and estimates – assigned to committees are highly partisan; under the conventions of parliamentary government, the government has a strong interest in ensuring that its legislation and programmes get passed. Other functions, however, are more non-partisan; those include independent investigations on behalf of the House as a whole.[20] These two different types of functions do not always work well when combined together in the same committee. Professor Franks goes on to point out that some committees can operate independently of the government, while others will work closely with and be influenced by the government. Each approach has strengths, and it depends to some extent on the subject matter and priorities of the government; the risks, however, are that the committee can become autonomous and bipartisan to the point of being ignored, on the one hand, or become an instrument in aid of the government, on the other.[21]

The argument has been made that Parliamentary Committees should restrict themselves to oversight functions – to making government accountable – and that they should not get involved in performing tasks or functions that should be done by governments. Certainly, in a traditional

17 Sutherland, SL, 'The Report of the Liaison Committee on the Effectiveness of House of Commons Committees' (1993) 44 Parliamentary Government, August, p 8.

18 *Op cit*, Franks, fn 3, p 163.

19 *Op cit*, Franks, fn 3, p 9.

20 *Op cit*, Franks, fn 3, p 164.

21 *Op cit*, Franks, fn 3, p 172.

parliamentary sense, the role of committees is more to monitor and review government action (or inaction) than it is to initiate or collaborate with government.

It has pointed out, however, that there is a distinctive place for Parliamentary Committees because of certain attributes. Peter O'Keeffe, Clerk Assistant (committees) in the Australian Senate, wrote in a 1992 article:

> The particular, unique attributes that committees bring to inquiry are party membership, electoral representation, political judgment, political influence, parliamentary power, privilege and witness immunity, and, theoretically at least, unrivalled political status. They lend themselves to certain types of inquiry in a way that weak, voluntary, secret, bureaucratic, judicial, academic or other non-Parliamentary Committees do not.[22]

Mr O'Keeffe points out that committees generally:

> ... are small, mobile, relatively informal, specialized, focused and designed for human interaction, both among the committee members themselves and collectively with witnesses, with a view to examining some important matters.[23]

In addition to operational flexibility, committees tend to have more time, fewer procedural restrictions and greater responsiveness than the legislature itself. Professor Franks makes the same point:

> Committees can do things which the House itself cannot. They can make investigations, during which they interrogate ministers and public servants, call expert witnesses, travel, and hire research staff; they can prepare reports which consider and accommodate the various interests and viewpoints of members and the public; they have the possibility of being non-partisan in a way the House rarely is. Committees can be a means by which members of Parliament can integrate their viewpoints into policy proposals, or act together to call the executive to account for its use of funds and authority. In almost every respect, the ideal of the committee stands in contrast to the reality of the House: they can be small and personal where the House is big and cold; the individual MP can be important in committee instead of being effaced by party discipline; the outcome of committee deliberations can be creative and exciting; committees can be non-partisan, sensitive, and subtle where the House is partisan, crude, and blunt; and above all, committees might, like those of the US Congress be powerful and efficient, where the House appears ineffective and cumbersome.[24]

---

22 O'Keeffe, P, 'The scope and function of Parliamentary Committees' (1992) 73 The Parliamentarian, October, 270, pp 270–71.

23 *Ibid*, p 270.

24 *Op cit*, Franks, fn 3, p 161.

REFORMS TO PARLIAMENTARY COMMITTEES

Committee structure

Various proposals have been put forward regarding the basic committee structure. This is also closely related to the number of Standing Committees, and is directly affected by the existence or absence of special or legislative committees. The 1985 McGrath Committee report recommended that the Standing Committee structure of the Canadian House of Commons reflect, as much as practicable, the organization of government; this led to a large number of committees, although it did not necessarily preclude committees having responsibility for more than one department. Such a scheme is reasonable in terms of specialist committees, although it does imply that the structure of the committee system is dictated by governmental considerations, rather than parliamentary ones.

There have also been suggestions that the committee structure should reflect the expenditure envelope system, which has some attraction if one agrees that financial oversight is a prime rationale for Parliamentary Committees. Between 1991 and 1994, the Standing Committees of the House were gathered into five broad 'envelopes', with the intention that membership and committee organization would be carried out within these envelopes. The system, however, does not appear to have resolved perennial problems or worked any better than the old system, and it was abandoned.

In Canada, with its extremely large geographic area, and distinct regions, suggestions have been made that Standing Committees be used to deal with regional issues. One proposal was to substitute five regional committees for existing Standing Committees:

> The current structuring of Standing Committees emphasizes the weakest aspect of MPs, their technical expertise, and neglects their greatest strength, their ability to represent their constituents and their region ... Ottawa does not lack technical capability and competence; what it lacks is an understanding or appreciation of the attitudes, feelings and aspirations of the regions.[25]

Number of committees

At present, there are 19 Standing (or Permanent) Committees in the Canadian House of Commons, as well as three Standing Joint Committees of the House and Senate. From time to time, Special (and Special Joint) Committees are

25 Crerar, A, 'Let Commons' committees work for the regions' (1992) 13 Policy Options 18, June, p 19.

established for specific studies. Over the years, the number of committees has fluctuated. As noted above, in the mid-1980s, there was a feeling that the committee structure should mirror the organization of government, which meant that the number of committees increased as the number of government departments proliferated. There was also a period of time – from about 1985 to 1993 – when a Legislative Committee was appointed for each Bill.

The larger the number of committees there are, generally the more meetings there are. This increases the demands on members' time, which is one of their scarcest commodities. It also means that there is more likelihood of conflicting meetings, requiring members to choose one committee over another and to miss other meetings.

Various proposals have been advanced regarding the number of committees. At one point in the early 1990s, there were suggestions that the number of Standing Committees be reduced to 10 or 11, with broader mandates, or that four or five 'super-committees', with large areas of study be created. In recent years, there have been on-going discussions in the Canadian Senate (which currently has 12 Standing Committees) about whether it would be better to have a large number of small committees dealing with relatively specific issues, or a few committees with broad mandates based on a particular policy field.

If there were fewer committees, it is suggested that increased use be made of sub-committees. Sub-committees have the advantage of generally being smaller, and composed of members with a particular interest or expertise in the subject matter. Moreover, since sub-committees generally cannot report directly to the House, there is usually not the same preoccupation that their composition reflect the party standings or that the government have a majority on them.

Number of committee positions

In the 35th Parliament, most of the 22 Standing and Standing Joint Committees of the House of Commons had 11 to 14 members. This meant that there were a large number of seats on committees that needed to be filled, an issue that is particularly acute for the government whip who generally wants to ensure that the government party can win any votes in committee.

The Canadian House of Commons currently has 301 members. The 1993 Liaison Committee report noted that about 60 of them are not available to sit on committees because of party leadership, House management or ministerial responsibilities. It compared this with the situation in other legislatures: the British House of Commons has 651 members who serve on 14 Standing Committees, as well as some legislative and special committees. The US Congress, with 435 members of the House of Representatives, limits the number of committees to 22. The German Bundestag's 662 legislators sit on 23 committees, while France's National Assembly, with 577 deputies, has only seven permanent commissions.

In Canada, there tends to be a nucleus of members on each committee who attend fairly regularly. In 1979, the Royal Commission on Financial Accountability and Reform (the Lambert Commission) discovered that half of all committee attendance was accounted for by only 42 MPs.[26] As Professor Franks has noted, 'The key problem is the lack of a resource of experienced independent-minded members'.[27] Not all members attach the same importance to committee work – some prefer to devote their time and energies to the House, constituency work, or other areas. Various studies and reports have concluded that many MPs are expected to serve on too many committees; moreover, Members who derive little satisfaction from service on committees devote less time to their committee assignments, which increases the burden on others.

In its 1993 report on committee effectiveness, the Liaison Committee said that 'committees work best when there are fewer places on committees than members',[28] and went on to suggest that there be 15 committees, with 10 members each. The McGrath Committee had also recommended smaller committees in its 1985 report, arguing that this would allow more time for probing and effective questioning, and that it would result in members valuing committee assignments more. Both the McGrath and Liaison Committees felt that membership on committees should not be obligatory; committees work best, in their views, if members want to serve on them, and if they value their committee memberships. They both looked favourably at the British House where positions on investigative committees are available for fewer than half the members, arguing there should be competition for committee places.

Part of the difficulty, however, is that, by tradition, the composition of committees reflects the party standings in the House of Commons or Senate. In addition, governments are anxious to keep control of committees, by ensuring that they have a majority of the seats on them. Whether these institutional constraints can be overcome – or minimized – remains to be seen.

In the case of many government members, they are often expected to serve on two, three or four committees, in addition to House duty and other responsibilities. The consequences of the government not having sufficient Members at committee meetings are appreciably greater than for opposition parties. Moreover, many government members are ineligible to serve on

26 Royal Commission on Financial Management and Accountability, Final Report, March 1979, p 398. See, also, Reid, JM, 'The back-bencher and the discharge of legislative responsibilities', in Neilson, WAW and MacPherson, JC (eds), *The Legislative Process in Canada*, 1978, Toronto: Butterworths.

27 *Op cit*, Franks, fn 3, p 181.

28 *Op cit*, Liaison Committee, fn 6, p 16.

committees, because they hold government or parliamentary offices, or are often unavailable to attend meetings because of other responsibilities; this, in turn, increases the demands on other government members to undertake committee responsibilities.

These problems are compounded in the Canadian House of Commons because of the concentration of committee meetings on certain days of the week: virtually all meetings are held on Tuesdays, Wednesday afternoons and evenings, and Thursday mornings and afternoons. Because of the size of Canada, members often spend many hours travelling back and forth to their constituencies, and many need to be in their constituencies at some point during the week. The result is that very few committee meetings are held on Mondays or Fridays.

Substitution of members

A perennial problem for Canadian Parliamentary Committees is the lack of continuity in membership. Part of this is attributable to the absence of a sense of 'ownership' among members towards their committee assignments. In addition to the many legitimate demands on their time, there often appears to be a lack of commitment towards committee work. Members are substituted on a regular basis, and often attend meetings only when pressed by their whips to be present. This 'revolving door' of members can severely inhibit work and effectiveness of committees; the frequent substitution of members contributes to instability or inconsistency and lack of continuity. As the Liaison Committee expressed it in its 1993 report:

> The widespread substitution of other members whenever a regular member of a committee is absent – a practice followed by all parties – has prevented committees from developing a collegial sense and ensured that committees remain under the control of party leaderships.[29]

The ideal solution would be to avoid substitutions as much as possible: this could be achieved by reducing the number of committee assignments of individual members and encouraging them to take their committee committee work more seriously. Where substitutions become necessary, various measures have been attempted. The McGrath Committee recommended that members be responsible for finding their own replacements, arguing that this would give members more responsibility and control over their parliamentary lives and lead them slowly but surely away from the concept that everything in the House is controlled by the whips and the House leadership. At present, members can arrange their own substitutes from a list filed with the clerk, but, more frequently, substitutions are effected by the party whips' offices based on the availability of members of the party. Since 1994, the Standing Orders

29 *Op cit*, Liaison Committee, fn 6, p 17.

also permit 'alternate members' to be appointed for Standing Committees, but it does not appear that this has led to any permanence in the members who are substituted on particular committees.

Committee chairs

The role of chair of a Parliamentary Committee is often one of leadership, and the success of the committee usually depends on the chair. Professor Wheare wrote in *Government by Committee* that a committee chair:

> ... represents [the members] if they need representation. He is Speaker on their behalf, whether it be in words of congratulation or condolence or whether it be in negotiation or in opposition to the claims or demands of other committees. In times of emergency, too, he usually acts on their behalf, seeking their confirmation for his actions later, while in normal times it is common for them to authorise him to act for them upon routine or even upon exceptional matters. In these and in many other ways, the one is made to speak or act for the many.[30]

Professor Franks has written that there is little possibility that the Standing Committees will become powerful independent bodies as long as they suffer from weak leadership:

> A committee cannot be better than its chairman. In Canada, the position has low prestige, it is used by the government as a stepping stone to unabashedly partisan positions, and its incumbents view the position as short term. Whatever hat the chairman wears in his role, he will have an eye cocked to pleasing the government: the rewards system of the House demands this.[31]

Various problems have been identified with respect to the chairing of House of Commons committees. Generally, the governing party decides who will chair which committees, and, while there is an election by the committee, its result is usually a foregone conclusion, at least in majority government situations. Governments often use the chairs of committees to reward certain members, or as a consolation for not being appointed to other positions. Tenure can be uncertain. There seldom seems to be much concern with the expertise of members, or a desire to promote long-serving members of a particular committee. This can be contrasted with the practice in the US Congress, where seniority is valued and legislators are encouraged to specialize and to concentrate their energies on particular committees.

Among the solutions that have been proposed are the election of chairs by secret ballot, and the payment of a salary supplement to chairs to reflect the additional time and work involved, and to encourage chairs to spend the

30 *Op cit*, Wheare, fn 10, pp 40–41.

31 *Op cit*, Franks, fn 3, p 165.

necessary time on committee organizational work. It has also been proposed that the chairs of committees be divided between government and opposition. The Standing Committees on Public Accounts and Scrutiny of Regulations have traditionally been chaired by a member from the Official Opposition, and, in the past, the Standing Committee on Management and Members' Services was also chaired by an opposition member; party standings on committees need not be adversely affected. In the Canadian Senate, the government and opposition negotiate a division of the chairing of committees at the beginning of each session, and this appears to work well. A similar scheme was apparently proposed in 1972 by a minority Liberal government, but rejected by the opposition at that time.

Use of committee time

As noted above, time is a very valuable commodity for politicians. The challenge is to make more effective use of committee time. Not only will members appreciate this, but it could help make committee work more attractive to them, and thereby help make committees more effective and influential.

The Liaison Committee, in its 1993 report, was in favour of the British tradition of placing greater emphasis on brief inquiries, rather than the mammoth royal commission type of inquiry that has been common in the past. It also emphasized that committee meetings need to be much better organized and structured; for instance, panels of witnesses could be set up so as to minimize duplication and facilitate more dialogue, and intensive days of hearings could be scheduled, rather than short meetings interspersed among other responsibilities. Most committees adopt a resolution allowing a reduced quorum for the hearing of witnesses; while this has certain advantages, it can also lead to difficulties, in terms of lack of continuity and so forth.

Strict limits have been proposed on the amount of time allotted to witnesses for their opening statements. Many committees already request that submissions be tabled in advance, so that they can be circulated to members prior to the appearance of the witness. It has also been suggested that the questioning of witnesses be by issue, with less concern about the order or length of time given to individual members or parties. Others have suggested that strict timelines be imposed on committee studies, as lengthy inquiries are not always the best use of committees' time.

Most of these measures require substantial organization and staff work, as well as some willingness on the part of members to change their attitudes.

Types of studies and inquiries

In its 1985 report, the McGrath Committee said:

> Committees would use their new authority to study the relevant government department in sufficient depth that a committee would become familiar with and be able to analyze and comment effectively on the government's future policy and expenditure plans. For example, with this broad mandate, a committee could examine the appropriateness of the legislation pertaining to, as well as the activities and expenditures, of a particular department.[32]

The intent of the McGrath Committee recommendation to give committees more autonomy in undertaking studies was to allow them to address broad policy issues and to give them more independence. In the spring of 1980, six parliamentary task forces had been appointed, each with a mandate to investigate a subject of high priority and to make recommendations at a time when they could have an influence on the formulation of government policy.[33] This experiment was reasonably successful, and it was hoped that changes to the Standing Orders would allow Standing Committees to duplicate their success.

Recent experience in Canada with royal commissions has been unsatisfactory – not only are such inquiries increasingly expensive, time consuming, and open to legal challenge, but their recommendations are often impractical and seldom implemented. It has been suggested – particularly in the Canadian Senate – that Parliamentary Committees could undertake much of the work currently given to such commissions. It has also been suggested that committees could be used much more by governments to provide an opportunity for public input before policies are adopted, such as reaction to White or Green Papers.

Peter O'Keeffe of the Australian Senate, has argued that Parliamentary Committees should not waste their valuable time and resources to investigate matters already under effective investigation elsewhere, or matters of technical complexity or requiring special knowledge. By the same token, he points out that matters involving criminality or confidentiality are seldom appropriate for study by Parliamentary Committees. He feels out that before a committee embarks on a study, it is essential that the members are interested or committed to it, and preferably such interest crosses party lines.

The forte of Parliamentary Committees, in Mr O'Keeffe's view, is in cross-matching of opinions and information for political implications and

32 Canada, House of Commons, Special Committee on Reform of the House of Commons, *Third Report*, June 1985, p 16.

33 Lever, NS, Plant Reynolds, B and Rosen, P, 'The parliamentary task forces: committees of the future' (1981) Canadian Parliamentary Rev, Spring, pp 15–20.

significance. As he writes, '... it is, of course, pointless for a Parliamentary Committee, comprised as it is of politicians, to investigate that which is not of political significance'.[34] Committee members are uniquely equipped to bring a political perspective to their assessment of an issue; far more than civil servants – or even Cabinet ministers – they can see the political implications of a proposal. Thus, matters requiring political sensitivity are good candidates for study by Parliamentary Committees.

Concerns have been expressed about committee agendas that are substantially determined by the government's legislative and policy priorities. Even though the work of such committees is likely to have more impact on government policy, there is a concern that if this is done on a systematic basis, it has the effect of co-opting the committee, and compromising the independence of the legislative branch. At the same time, if committees pursue their own agenda, there is no assurance that governments will be interested in or adopt their recommendations. According to Peter O'Keeffe:

> A committee which regularly accepts references directly from ministers risks being used, captured by a ministerial agenda and a desire not to criticise the hand that is apparently feeding it. Worse still, it masks the truth by giving the appearance of independent purpose, and abuses the legitimate expectations of the public ... I would have thought that committees should actively seek out those very matters which ministers least want them to look at.[35]

As in so many things, it is probably necessary to achieve an appropriate balance between these conflicting approaches.

It is not always easy to measure the effectiveness of Parliamentary Committees; there is no simple scale to measure influence or impact. Yet, some assessment must be undertaken in order to determine the effectiveness of committees, and to guide committees in deciding what work or activities to pursue. The Select Committee on Procedure of the British House of Commons tabled a report in October 1990 entitled *The Working of the Select Committee System,* it which it applied four yardsticks:

(1) the success in holding ministers and officials to account;

(2) putting valuable information into the public domain and thereby contributing to greater public understanding;

(3) contributing to more informed consideration of important matters in the House and in the public forums; and

(4) influencing, directly or indirectly, the government's actions.[36]

34 *Op cit*, O'Keeffe, fn 22, p 272.

35 *Op cit*, O'Keeffe, fn 22, p 272.

36 UK, House of Commons, Select Committee on Procedure, *Second Report, The Working of the Select Committee System*, October 1990.

Consideration of legislation

Various suggestions have been made in the past that the House of Commons should refer Bills to committees after first reading, rather than waiting until second reading. For instance, in a 1993 report, the House of Commons Standing Committee on House Management recommended such a change to the legislative process:

> We believe that all Bills should be referred to a Legislative Committee directly after they are introduced in the House. Bills would then be studied by the committee, which would effectively be engaged in a form of pre-study. The Bill would not have been voted on in principle, and, therefore, amendments would not be inadmissible on the basis that [they] went beyond the principle or scope of the Bill. Members would thus have much more flexibility in terms of reviewing and finetuning legislation.[37]

New Zealand has had some notable successes in this area, and in 1994 Standing Orders of the Canadian House were amended to allow such a procedure. Under Standing Order 73, a Bill can be referred to a committee before second reading. Such a motion can only be moved by a minister immediately after the commencement of second reading of a public Bill. The debate on the motion to refer the Bill is subject to certain conditions: the order of speaking is set out, the motion is not able to be amended, and no member can speak more than once or for longer than 10 minutes. After three hours of debate, the Speaker must interrupt the proceedings and the question shall be decided without further debate or amendment.

The Bill can be referred to a Standing, Special or Legislative Committee. Once the Bill is reported back to the House, provision is made for report stage: amendments can be proposed and are subject generally to the same rules as at a traditional report stage. When report stage has been completed, a second reading vote is held, but there is no debate. The Bill then proceeds to the usual third reading. The new process is explained in new Standing Order 76 (10), which provides:

> (10) The report stage of a Bill pursuant to this Standing Order shall be deemed to be an integral part of the second reading stage of the Bill. When a Bill has been concurred on and read a second time in accordance with the procedures set forth in this Standing Order, it shall be set down for a third reading and passage at the next sitting of the House.

The advantages cited in favour of this form of 'pre-study' are that it allows the government to hear public reaction before second reading stage, party positions may not be so firmly entrenched, committees can have more influence in terms of the Bill, and members are not as restricted in terms of the

37 Canada, House of Commons, Standing Committee on House Management, *Eighty-first Report*, 1 April 1993.

types of amendments that they can propose as they are after second reading. It has also been suggested that its use could make second reading more focused and less protracted, or, as under the 1994 Standing Order, basically eliminate the need for a second reading debate.

The pre-study procedure under the Standing Orders 76 was not used very frequently in the 35th Parliament – motions to refer Bills were tabled on 19 occasions, and adopted on 16. Part of the reason is that this is an alternative process for dealing with legislation – it is not the norm, as was proposed by the House Management Committee. More importantly, however, opposition parties argued that in practice the new procedure did not really open up the process appreciably, and that a motion to refer a Bill to a committee before second reading was effectively used by the government as a form of time allocation as it permits a maximum three hour debate. It is also likely only certain kinds of Bills lend themselves to such a procedure: if the parties have already staked out their positions or if the government (or civil service) are unwilling to alter the basic legislative scheme, the chances of success are reduced.

Concerns were also expressed about the elimination of second reading debate, and the absence of any formal opportunity to debate the principle of a Bill. There was (and is) some concern that this will make it more difficult for opposition members to criticize a Bill, particularly if they have been involved in trying to improve the Bill in committee. At the same time, for many years, the Canadian Senate engaged in the pre-study of Commons Bills; while this practice fell into disuse in the last decade, there are indications that it will be revived.

Concerns have been expressed that any new process should be used to streamline the legislative process, not to add another layer to it. By the same token, there have been proposals that report stage in the House of Commons be eliminated or severely restricted. Under the current Standing Orders, amendments to Bills are supposed to be moved during committee consideration. After the Bill is reported back to the House, however, there is a report stage, at which members who did not sit on the committee have an opportunity to move amendments. The Speaker has some discretion in accepting amendments – he or she is supposed to reject amendments that were dealt with by the committee, or which could have been presented in committee. The practice, however, is that many amendments are saved for the House, where they are more likely to receive attention. The result is a lengthy legislative process, and scope for duplication. Proposals have been made that amendments to Bills only be dealt with by committees, and that, if necessary, Bills be referred back to committee by the House rather than using valuable House time. If changes were made in this area, they would probably have the effect of enhancing the role and importance of committees in the legislative process.

Drafting of legislation

The 1995 McGrath Committee report argued that Standing Committees should be able to play an important part in influencing policy through the legislative process, and that they should be become critical components in the consultation process that takes place before legislation is introduced. One way of achieving this is to have Bills prepared or drafted by Parliamentary Committees.

In January 1993, the Liberal Party of Canada unveiled a plan for the House of Commons and Electoral Reform entitled *Reviving Parliamentary Democracy*. This plan argued that there needed to be increased involvement of parliamentarians at the early stage of legislative process:

> Under the present practice, the real legislative process is virtually complete even before a Bill is given first reading in the House of Commons. Ministers and their officials conduct extensive interdepartmental and intergovernmental discussions and often consult the private sector as well in preparing a Bill. The legislation presented to the House is often the product of extensive compromise and balancing. Since all of the discussion is private, however, there is no real assurance that all parties [whose] interests are at stake have been adequately canvassed – or even consulted at all.[38]

The Liberals noted that, once a Bill is presented to Parliament, the government often becomes obstinate about its provisions: 'As a result, debate on controversial legislation is usually characterized by negativism, unnecessary repetitiveness and even destructive oratorical pyrotechnics.' It was noted that it was common practice in earlier times for committees to be appointed to prepare a Bill, and urged the revival of such a process:

> A committee appointed to prepare legislation can carry out all of [the] required interdepartmental, intergovernmental and public consultation necessary and *can do so openly*, thereby providing Canadians with greater assurance of even-handed propriety. These consultations would be far more meaningful than those often now carried out on legislation because the committee would not be confined by its government supporters being constrained by orders to defend an already defined position.
>
> Once the Bill is prepared, since it is the creature of a committee, rather than of the government, there would be no question of any vote on the Bill being a question of confidence and, therefore, no need for the Whips to be applied on any such vote.
>
> Debate on subsequent stages of a Bill drafted by a committee is not likely to lend itself to bitter partisanship and the broadly constructed committee hearings now held after second reading would be completely unnecessary ...
>
> Eventually, virtually all legislation could be initiated by committee. The process of parliamentarians, bureaucrats and the public openly collaborating

38 Liberal Party of Canada, *Reviving Parliamentary Democracy*, January 1993.

> may, however, take some time and experience before it becomes a smooth one. It would, therefore, seem sensible to begin the process with a few – perhaps a half-dozen – legislative initiatives in the first year, the subject-matter of the legislation to be agreed upon by the parties in the House and with the number being increased each year after.

When the Liberal Party came to power, they introduced amendments to the Standing Orders to appoint or instruct a Standing, Special or Legislative Committee to prepare and bring in a Bill. A motion to this effect may be moved by a Minister under Government Orders, and the debate on the motion can last for up to 90 minutes. The Speaker shall then interrupt debate, and put all questions necessary to dispose of the motion without further debate or amendment. No Member may speak more than once, or for more than 10 minutes. Amendments to the motion can be proposed.

Once the committee has reported back, a minister may propose a motion to concur in its report. Such a motion is to be taken up under government orders, and can be the subject of time allocation proceedings under Standing Order 78. The adoption of such a motion constitutes an order to bring in a Bill based on the committee report.

Once the Bill is introduced, there must be three sitting days before it is set down for consideration at second reading. It is provided that there will be no debate or amendment at second reading for such Bills. Once the Bill receives second reading, however, it follows the usual course of being referred to a standing, special or legislative committee, report stage and third reading.

The committee is not required to produce actual wording. Standing Order 68(5) provides:

> (5) A committee appointed or instructed to prepare and bring in a Bill shall, in its report, recommend the principles, scope and general provisions of the said Bill and may, if it deems it appropriate, but not necessarily, include recommendations regarding legislative wording.

Thus, the committee does not have to draft a formal Bill or provide legal language, but it is expected to provide instructions to the drafters. Concerns have been expressed that, if the committee does not provide actual wording, it will be dependent on what the government drafters come up with. There is the possibility that the Bill that is subsequently introduced may differ from that envisaged by the committee.

Various commentators had expressed doubts about the ability to commit to draft legislation. There are well established processes in government departments for proposed Bills to be developed, reviewed and approved. While these processes may be cumbersome and time-consuming, they do serve a purpose. The committee will not necessarily have access to the expertise and advice that is available to the cabinet. Problems could arise – both with respect to drafting the Bill on the basis of the committee's instructions, and the policies themselves – as has happened in the case of Private Members' Bills.

There is also some concern that as committees operate on the basis of what the majority decides, opposition members could be manipulated or 'co-opted' by the new process. That is, by being on the committee that prepares a Bill they will appear to be involved in the development of a policy, and could be placed in a position where they have to support the Bill.

This procedure of instructing a committee to prepare and bring in a Bill was first used in 1994 when the Standing Committee on Procedure and House Affairs was asked to review legislation involving the readjustment of electoral boundaries. While a statute had been in place since the early 1960s, it had never functioned very smoothly, and the commencement of the most recent attempt at redistribution had led to considerable dissatisfaction. After several months of study, the committee reported back with a completely drafted Bill, which was adopted by the government with only a few technical changes. The Bill was passed quickly by the House of Commons, but ran into opposition in the Senate, and died on the *Order Paper* when Parliament was prorogued. Even though the two opposition parties in the House opposed specific aspects of the Bill, they strongly supported the initiative. Generally, there was a feeling that the drafting of the Bills by a Parliamentary Committee was a positive experience, and holds considerable potential for the future.

This new process is unlikely to be appropriate for all Bills, and, as noted above, it is somewhat contrary to the division of responsibilities between the legislative and executive branches. In a parliamentary system of government, the drafting of Bills is usually seen as a function of the executive – rather than of the legislature – unlike a congressional-type system of government. At the same time, until fairly recently, most legislation in the Canadian Parliament was tabled by Private Members rather than by government ministers. There is considerable support for a more transparent and accessible legislative process, and for more involvement of individual parliamentarians.

Powers of committees

Committees in the Canadian House of Commons already have extensive powers. Standing Order 108(1)(a) provides:

> Standing Committees shall be severally empowered to examine and enquire into all such matters as may be referred to them by the House, to report from time to time and to print a brief appendix to any report, after the signature of the chairman, containing such opinions or recommendations, dissenting from the report or supplementary to it, as may be proposed by committee members, and except when the House otherwise orders, to send for persons, papers and records, to sit while the House is sitting, to sit during periods when the House

stands adjourned, to sit jointly with other Standing Committees, to print from day to day such papers and evidence as may be ordered by them, and to delegate to subcommittees all or any of their powers except the power to report directly to the House.

The McGrath Committee recommended in 1985 that legislation be introduced empowering the House of Commons to impose a fine for contempt of Parliament. Another suggestion is that committees should be allowed to continue their work notwithstanding a prorogation or even a dissolution. While such proposals would increase the independence of Parliamentary Committees, they run contrary to the principle that committees are the creations of the House, which must retain a certain degree of control.

Proposals have also been made that committees be given more discretion to allow the electronic media to film or broadcast their proceedings.[39] Since the early 1990s, there has been a dedicated committee room for broadcasting: committees meeting in this room have their proceedings taped, and these are broadcast on CPaC, a television channel operated by a consortium of cable companies that broadcasts the proceedings of the House of Commons live, as committee meetings and other unfiltered events of public interest or importance. The audio portion of committee meetings can also be recorded, and is broadcast throughout the parliamentary precincts. Broadcasting makes Parliamentary Committees more accessible to the public, and highlights the important work of committees and time spent by parliamentarians.

Miscellaneous proposals

A multitude of other reforms have been proposed for Parliamentary Committees. Among these are the following:

- One of the main roles of Parliament is to vote on the expenditure of moneys for the government, and to hold the government accountable for its spending. Except at a very general level, this requires fairly detailed and technical scrutiny if it is to be done responsibly. While Parliamentary Committees are charged with reviewing the spending estimates of government departments and agencies, this is often not undertaken in a thorough or systematic way. In recent years, attempts have been made to strengthen the estimates process, by breaking it up into a review of future priorities, the review of spending plans, and an assessment of whether targets have been achieved. In April 1997, a subcommittee on the Business of Supply tabled a report with a comprehensive set of recommendations for improving the supply process, but this report had not been dealt with prior to the general election. As the Royal Commission on Financial

39 See, for instance, *Watching the House at Work,* Ninth Report of the Standing Committee on Elections, Privileges, Procedure and Private Members' Business, December 1989.

Management and Accountability concluded in 1979, 'the key to the House of Commons assuming a more effective and influential role in financial management and accountability lies in its committee system'.[40]

- The Liaison Committee's 1993 report argued that, 'in order to ensure that committees have a sense of direction and a corporate memory, they should have a small, dedicated core staff. Although committee staff should have the prospect of continuous employment, committees should review their performance at the beginning of each session to ensure that they were working effectively'.[41] Appropriate staffing is essential if Parliamentary Committees are to function well; this includes clerks, researchers, and support staff. Whether these people should be hired by the committee, or provided to the committee by the House of Commons, the Library of Parliament, or another entity is a subject of debate. Certainly, US Congressional Committees have large professional staffs, and this undoubtedly contributes to their strengths; at the same time, concerns have been expressed that permanent staff can control committees to the exclusion of the politicians.
- In its 1993 report, the Liaison Committee suggested that it would be useful if committees were to make a conscious effort to identify their objectives and prepare a work plan when undertaking a new task. It was also suggested that committees would benefit from preparing an annual report of the work undertaken and in progress, the reasons for doing the work and assessing what success they had in realizing their goals.
- There is provision under the Standing Orders of the House of Commons for committees to request a comprehensive response from the government to a committee report, and the government then has 180 days in which to respond. Unfortunately, these 'comprehensive' responses are often very cursory, and Speakers have taken the position that it is not for them to assess the sufficiency of the response. Implementing measures to ensure that complete and considered responses are provided would be beneficial. It has also been pointed out that Standing Committees, because of their continued existence, have the power to follow up government responses, but seldom do, partly because of the lack of continuity in committee membership; this too is an avenue to be explored by committees.

  The Liaison Committee recommended that committee reports and government responses be used as occasions for brief debates in the House.

40 Quoted in *op cit*, Franks, fn 3, p 171.

41 *Op cit*, Liaison Committee, fn 6, p 21.

- Proposals have been made to increase influence of committees, to engage the interest of media and to stimulate public interest and debate. For instance, it has been suggested that short, sharp reports should be encouraged, joint hearings held with other committees, meetings arranged with US and other counterparts, carefully organized collections of testimony published, inviting non-parliamentarians to sit on a committee as *ex officio* members, and increasing co-ordination among Standing Committees in terms of their work and tabling of reports.

Committees should make increased use of new technologies. For instance, teleconferencing allows committees to hear from people in different places, without the expense of the committee travelling or paying for witnesses to come to them. Although systems have been in place for teleconferencing over the last few years in Canada, it appears that, while some committees have made extensive use of such systems, others have not.

CONCLUSIONS

When a new committee system was established in 1968, Members of the Canadian House of Commons on both sides of the House held high hopes for a substantial strengthening of their influence through work on committees which could examine issues of critical national importance. After a flurry of activity in the early 1970s, disillusionment set in. This pattern has repeated itself after other attempts at reform. As the above discussion illustrates, there is no shortage of proposals to improve the committee system. Attempts continue to be made since, in the words of Professor Franks, 'committees offer the beguiling prospect of a stronger, more independent role for Parliament'.[42]

Parliamentary Committees do have enormous potential. With the increasing complexity of government and legislation, particularly in an era of fiscal restraint, committees assist the House to perform its oversight functions and to influence government policy.

Members of Parliament are more experienced than in the past, and many bring valuable experience, expertise and perspective to their jobs. The public expects more of their elected representatives, and committees are one means of addressing these expectations.

As Peter O'Keeffe expresses it:

> Through their mobility, specialization, power, immunity, status, political skill and media attention, committees can draw to themselves information and confidences which others will not obtain.[43]

42 *Op cit*, Franks, fn 2, p 161.

43 *Op cit*, O'Keeffe, fn 22, p 272.

As part of the political process, committees can provide input, help build consensus, help educate and inform the public, and provide leadership, especially on issues that have not become bogged down in party political entrenchment.

It is inherent in our system that governments will seek to control committees. They want to avoid embarrassment and try to ensure support for their policies. At times, it may not be so much the cabinet as bureaucrats, who want to avoid interference by Parliamentary Committees or are wary of alternative sources of advice. As Professor Franks has written:

> ... many of the actors involved – ministers and civil servants, highly partisan politicians, the media with their critical bias, and all the many critics of Canadian governance [–] do not mind seeing the committees fail. There are not many left who really want the committees to succeed.[44]

A system of specialist committees has long been established in Canada, unlike some other parliamentary systems. There have been some notable successes, but it is probably fair to say that committees have not always lived up to their potential. Part of the difficulty is in determining the proper role or function for committees in a parliamentary environment. Governments are responsible to the House of Commons, and it is neither feasible nor appropriate that committees should become partners with government in the formulation of policy. Parliamentary Committees have an essential advisory and monitoring role to play in assisting the executive and holding it rigorously to account. This is not to say, however, that the expertise and political abilities of parliamentarians could not be better used by Parliaments and governments.

Committees have to cease being miniature Parliaments, with all the baggage of a legislature, and become more creative. Some of the challenges are structural or institutional: the Canadian House of Commons has difficulty in creating non-partisan committees, and it also has a history of very high turnover of members. In the view of Professor Franks, Canadian committees fail because almost all business which comes before the House is treated as partisan because party lines are rigid, and because these divisions and rigidities extend to committees; committees continue to be dominated by the government.

Procedurally, a great deal has been done in the Canadian House of Commons to enhance the role and importance of committees. As always, changes and refinements are possible. Fundamentally, though, the success of the committee system depends on the members of the House. Only they can make it work. It is their collective responsibility to assert the rights of committees, and to devote the necessary time and energy to them. If the will is there, the future of Parliamentary Committees will be bright.

44 Franks, CES, 'Comments on the Report of the Liaison Committee' (1993) 44 Parliamentary Government, August, p 6.

CHAPTER 21

THE HISTORY OF THE COMMITTEE SYSTEM ON THE WESTMINSTER MODEL[1]

Giles Radice, MP, United Kingdom

The use of committees by the United Kingdom Parliament, and its predecessors, has hardly ever been systematic: its history has been one of the haphazard adaptation of existing forms to suit the exigencies of the moment. Its principal feature – the distinction between Standing Committees, which debate public legislation, and Select Committees, which scrutinise the activity of government – is one which has arisen partly as a result of historical accident, although it has become overlain with elements of a theoretical justification drawn from the principle of ministerial responsibility, and the need for Parliament to scrutinise the exercise of that responsibility.

Committees of some form appear to have existed in the earliest Parliaments: there is evidence of eight committees being established in the Parliament of 1340.[2] But little is known about them until the mid-16th century. By 1536, the practice of committing Bills to Select Committees was described as if it were routine.[3]

Committees were often appointed for broader discussions, which might lead to the drafting of a Bill; they could be appointed in order to meet with a similar Committee in the House of Lords, in order to discuss disputed points between the two Houses, or to attend the King or the Queen.[4] They were nominated by the House, and met separately from it.

COMMITTEES OF THE WHOLE HOUSE

Among the most significant committees were those to discuss grants of taxation: such committees are known to have existed in 1547, when the surviving Journals begin. In 1593, the business of supply was committed to a Committee so large it was effectively a Committee of the Whole House, and met in the Chamber itself. Thereafter, such a large committee was always used

1 Apart from remarks at the outset and conclusion, this note covers committees in the House of Commons only.

2 Sayles, GO, *The King's Parliament of England*, 1975, p 112.

3 Lehmberg, SE, *The Reformation Parliament*, 1970, p 238.

4 Dean, D, *Law-making and Society in late Elizabethan England*, 1996, pp 23–25; Elton, GR, *The Parliament of England 1559–81*, 1986, pp 96–111.

for supply business. Far from allowing opposition to be expressed more freely, as was once argued, the main motive for doing so appears to have been to allow government spokesmen more easily to rebut inconvenient arguments as they arose. The practice was soon extended to other matters: in 1604, when no committee was appointed for supply, two large committees were appointed instead for grievances, in a process stage-managed by the government. Soon after, the House abandoned going through the motions of nominating committees of this sort, and they were acknowledged (by 1607) as Committees of the Whole House.[5]

The practice of appointing a set of Standing Committees (or 'Grand Committees') was a separate, but closely related, development of the early 17th century. These were given broad authority to pursue a set of particular issues; although all members could participate in them, unlike a Committee of the Whole House they met outside the House. There were four: for grievances; religion; courts of justice; and trade. In the early 17th century, the committees occasionally functioned as a device by which elements within government could attempt to co-opt parliamentarians into programmes of reform. They easily became confused, however, with Committees of the Whole House, and were effectively assimilated to them.[6] After the restoration of the monarchy in 1660, they ceased to exist except in the formal order for their appointment at the beginning of each session (a practice which was not abandoned until 1832).

COMMITTEES TO CONSIDER BILLS

It appears to have been in the 1690s that the practice of committing public Bills to Select Committees fell into disfavour; why it did so remains mysterious, although it may be because of the prominence in the 1690s of financial bills. By the early 18th century, most public Bills were committed to Committee of the Whole House.[7]

By the mid-19th century, the additional political interest that came with parliamentary reform was producing developments in Parliament that made some change to this pattern essential. The legislative ambitions of increasingly interventionist governments had to be catered for, and competed with the growing clamour of reform-minded Private Members to get their own measures on to the statute book.[8]

5 Lambert, S, 'Procedure in the House of Commons in the early Stuart period' (1980) English Historical Rev, p xcv.

6 Lambert, S, 'Committees, religion and parliamentary encroachment on royal authority in early Stuart England' (1990) English Historical Rev 414, January, pp 60–95.

7 Thomas, PDG, *The House of Commons in the Eighteenth Century*, 1970.

8 Ramm, A, 'The parliamentary context of Cabinet government, 1868–74' (1984) English Historical Rev, pp 739–69.

Thomas Erskine May's proposal of 1848, to establish a system of 'Grand Committees', or Standing Committees with a core, specialist membership, to which Bills were committed, harked back to the 17th century Grand Committees. The idea eventually bore fruit as the basis of Gladstone's strategy against the disruptive tactics of the Irish members demanding home rule. In 1882, two Standing Committees were set up, one for law, courts and legal proceedings, and the other for trade, shipping and manufacture; they had a permanent membership of from 60 to 80 members, and 15 more were added for individual Bills. Their procedure was modelled on that of a Select Committee, rather than that of a Committee of the Whole House. From the start, such committees were supposed to deal with non-controversial Bills, but the demands of increasing business meant that there was constant pressure to refer more and more to them. The system was remodelled, and incorporated into Standing Orders in 1907, when four committees were established (including one specifically for Scottish Bills, dominated by Scottish members, and one reserved for Private Members' Bills). Over the following years, the number of committees were expanded, and the membership of each reduced. In 1945, the Labour government proposed to refer all Bills to Standing Committees except for very minor ones and Bills of 'first class constitutional importance'. These changes were incorporated into Standing Orders in 1947, creating essentially the system of Standing Committees that exists today.[9] The most recent reforms have been to give the Scottish and Welsh Grand Committees wider powers to consider Bills, question ministers and to debate subjects of importance to their respective countries.

SELECT COMMITTEES

Once most public legislation had been removed from Select Committees, they were confined to private legislation and detailed inquiry into particular topics and subjects. Such committees of inquiry were popular during the 18th century, particularly as a device of opposition attacks on Sir Robert Walpole and other ministers.

Eighteenth century Select Committees were appointed as and when required, for the examination of particular issues, or inquiry into specific abuses when they emerged. But, the reform debate of the late 18th and early 19th centuries created pressure for a more systematic use of committees, to provide more constant scrutiny of an expanding government. Finance Committees and *ad hoc* committees into departmental expenditure were appointed fairly regularly in the early 19th century. Ministers regularly opposed the latter because the breadth of their terms of reference meant that

9 Higgins, GM, *Standing Committees of the House of Commons*, 1952, Oxford University, B Litt thesis.

they quickly became involved in policy matters, as much as the detail of administration and expenditure and could act as an irritating forum for policy debate.[10] Gladstone's government agreed to the establishment of a Select Committee of Public Accounts in 1861, specifically to examine the audited accounts of the government, only because it was precluded from commenting on policy.[11]

The Public Accounts Committee (PAC) soon proved its worth, and pleased Treasury Ministers, in scrutinising the way in which money had been spent. It did not make ministers any happier, however, about exposing the Estimates, their expenditure plans, to the detailed scrutiny of a committee. Examination of planned expenditure would, it was felt, be more likely to draw in policy matters and threaten the responsibility of ministers. Nevertheless, ministers were gradually forced into accepting committees to examine the Estimates by the difficulty of managing debates on supply in the House itself. Debates on supply in Committee of the Whole House threatened to take up much of the time of the House, but by limiting the number of days spent on supply from 1896 governments were open to the charge that they were preventing the House from properly considering the Estimates. A Committee on the Estimates was the obvious answer, but was resisted for many years. In 1903, such a committee was recommended by a National Expenditure Committee but it was not actually set up until 1912, and it was abandoned at the onset of the First World War. Another committee, the National Expenditure Committee, was established in 1917, with 26 members and a power to make subcommittees, with rather more general terms of reference, to look at possible economies (as long as they were 'consistent with ... policy'), and to propose a permanent system for the examination of the estimates. Concern to ensure a proper system for doing this joined with interest (reflected in the Haldane Committee on the machinery of government of 1918) in creating a system of Parliamentary Committees which could supervise the work of each government department. An Estimates Committee was appointed, in line with the National Expenditure Committee's recommendations, in 1921, although the government acquiesced in it only reluctantly. Though it survived until 1939, it failed to make much impact until the late 1930s. As in the First World War, the Estimates Committee lapsed in the Second. A National Expenditure Committee replaced it, developing a departmentally related subcommittee system which was adopted by the Estimates Committee when it was revived in 1946.[12]

The concern about the usurpation by committees of policy matters held up the development of a fully fledged system of departmental committees such

10 Basil Chubb, *The Control of Public Expenditure*, 1952, p 25.

11 *Ibid*, p 35.

12 Johnson, N, 'Select committees and administration', in Walkland, SA, *The House of Commons in the Twentieth Century*, 1979, Oxford: OUP.

as that suggested by Haldane. But, by the 1960s, it was coming to seem out-of-date, and a concern that Parliament was being eclipsed by the executive increased the pressure for institutional reform. In 1965, the Procedure Committee recommended the widening of the terms of reference of the Estimates Committee so that it could examine how the departments carried out their responsibilities, with specialist subcommittees. The reforms of 1966 and after did not quite achieve this. Some departmentally related committees were established (Agriculture, Education and Science, Scottish Affairs, Overseas Aid) and some were set up covering broad subject areas (Race Relations and Immigration; Science and Technology). In 1971, the Estimates Committee was replaced with a Expenditure Committee which was intended to provide a rather more coherent structure; but difficulties with this brought a Procedure Committee review, and the establishment in 1979 of the more coherent system, based on government departments, that currently exists.[13]

Standing beside the departmentally related Select Committees, and the Committee on Public Accounts, other scrutiny committees have been established from time to time to address apparent gaps in the House's review of legislation and government expenditure. The Select Committee on Nationalised Industries was first established in 1951 because these were seen as insulated from both commercial and parliamentary pressure to achieve good value for money. The Committee (which had been established afresh in each Parliament, rather than being enshrined in Standing Orders) was not re-appointed in 1979 and its work was subsumed into that of the departmentally related committees. The Select Committee on the Parliamentary Commissioner for Administration (PCA) was set up in 1967, to examine the reports of the Parliamentary Commissioner, established under an Act of that year. A similar structure was adopted when the Select Committee on Standards and Privileges was given power to examine the reports of the Parliamentary Commissioner for Standards (in 1995), although the relationship between this committee and the Parliamentary Commissioner is much closer than that between the PCA and the ombudsman.

Three Select Committees have been established to exercise semi-legislative functions. A Select Committee to scrutinise delegated legislation was recommended in 1932, but not created until 1944 (in 1973, it became part of a Joint Committee with the Lords). The UK's entry into the European Community provoked concern that decisions taken by the Council of Ministers could have direct legislative effect without proper parliamentary scrutiny and so a Committee was established to sift through draft legislation from the Council of Ministers. A further committee, the Deregulation Committee, was established in 1994 to review deregulation orders under the Deregulation and Contracting Out Act 1994.

13 See First Report from the Select Committee on Procedure, HC (1977–78) 588.

This chapter should have demonstrated that the history of the committee system has been one of evolution by fits and starts, rather than by steady progress. Parliament's willingness to use and reuse forms as they become appropriate can be seen in the appointment of a Joint Committee on Parliamentary Privilege made in the last days before the summer recess. Committees dealing with technical matters like the Joint Committee on Consolidation, etc, Bills are regular features of the parliamentary landscape, but a Joint Committee to consider a particular subject is not. There was a Joint Committee on House of Lords Reform in the early 1960s; another in the late 1980s considered Private Bill procedure; it may be decades before there another; it is equally possible that, in five years time, a chapter like this will be forced to devote itself to explaining the evolution of the many Joint Committees to consider parliamentary reform set up since 1997.

CHAPTER 22

THE PURPOSE, FUNCTION AND OPERATION OF COMMITTEES

Giles Radice, MP, United Kingdom

What are committees for? In 1978, the Select Committee on Procedure described them as not an end in themselves, but 'a means to secure greater surveillance of the executive by Parliament'.[1] The purpose has not changed. The committee also noted, in words which many will find applicable today:

> The present committee system has for the most part developed in response to the need to relieve the pressure of business on the floor of the House or in response to new obligations or to demands for the House to perform new functions involving detailed investigation which are unsuited to a large assembly. The system which we have inherited is unplanned and unstructured.[2]

The House has continued to respond to new pressures by adapting the committee system by considering the functions which each new committee or type of committee has to fulfil, rather than by trying to contain new committees within some pre-ordained, logically structured system. Although the committee system in the present House of Commons is perhaps not as unstructured as the Procedure Committee implied, this evolutionary development makes it hard to draw up any scheme; exceptions and anomalies will always abound.

The House of Commons operates two principal types of committee: the Standing Committee and the Select Committee. There are other types of Committee extant – Joint Committees including members from Lords and Commons, and Committees on Private Bills and Hybrid Bill Committees for example, but these are relatively arcane.

Standing Committees include the Grand Committees; the Welsh and Scottish Grand Committees[3] provide a forum for debate on matters of particular importance to those countries, and hold second reading debates on bills of peculiar Scottish or Welsh interest (after these debates the House decides forthwith the question that the Bill be read a second time). But, the ordinary run of Standing Committees deal with the scrutiny of legislation; their function is to take a Bill which has passed its second reading and consider it in detail, amending it when necessary, or to consider delegated

1 First Report from the Select Committee on Procedure, HC (1977–78) 588, para 1.12.

2 *Ibid*, para 1.10.

3 There is also provision for a Northern Ireland Grand Committee.

legislation, or European Community documents. Business in the European Standing Committees is closely linked to decisions made by the Select Committee on European Legislation.

The Chairmen of Standing Committees are appointed by the Speaker, and, since Standing Committees are governed by many of the formal rules which apply in the Chamber, they exercise analogous powers to the Speaker. All proceedings take place in public (committees have the power to order that 'strangers do withdraw', but, like the House itself, they do not use it). Standing Committees report to the House, but do so by reporting the Bill they were established to consider, either with or without amendment, or, in the case of delegated legislation, by making a report that they have considered the instrument. The formal Minutes of Proceedings may appear some while after the Standing Committee meets, but proceedings are recorded by *Hansard* and published the day after each sitting, and an informal indication of the previous day's decisions taken on each amendment to a Bill is circulated with the vote.

As far as Bills are concerned, in principle, the painstaking scrutiny of each clause, and of each line of each clause can not only tease out points of political difference but can, and frequently does, reveal technical weaknesses in drafting. However, Standing Committee procedures have their disadvantages. The committee may concentrate debate on particular parts of a Bill, and, either because a guillotine is imposed, or because of informal agreements between the whips, find that there is not sufficient time for consideration of other significant aspects. In Standing Committees, as in the House as a whole, member speaks to member; although civil servants are present to brief ministers and pressure groups may pass notes to the opposition, these outsiders have no direct influence on the proceedings, and their cases cannot be tested directly. Standing Committees are re-constituted afresh for each Bill; while this can (or could) enable the Committee of Selection to assemble the group of members best suited to consider each Bill, it means that Standing Committees have no collective memory or accumulated expertise. Any member may attend and speak at a Standing Committee on Delegated Legislation, but the committee has no power to amend the delegated legislation before it, or to pass a motion other than the formal record that the committee has considered the instrument.

While the purpose of Standing Committees is, in general, limited to the consideration of specific pieces of legislation, Select Committees in the House of Commons perform a variety of functions; broadly speaking, they can be divided into those dealing with the internal affairs of the House; those which oversee the work of an independent officer, such as the Public Accounts Committee and the Select Committee on Standards and Privileges; those which scrutinise legislation – the European Legislation Committee, the Deregulation Committee, the Joint and Select Committees on Statutory Instruments and the Joint Committee on Consolidation of Bills, Etc, and those which deal with the wider business of government – the departmental Select Committees.

In contrast to Standing Committees, Select Committees are usually appointed for an entire Parliament, the membership changes only very slowly (indeed, many members of a Select Committee in one Parliament may return to the same committee after an election), and, over time, each committee will develop its own *modus operandi.* Each Select Committee will choose its own chairman, and although there is usually an informal understanding about the party from which the chairman will come and, indeed, who will take the chair, the committee need not abide by these understandings (and there have been some notable upsets in the past). The findings and recommendations of Select Committees are submitted to the House as printed reports. The Minutes of Proceedings relating to each report are printed with them, and record any disagreements which could not be resolved informally. Most Select Committees take some evidence, although the frequency with which evidence is taken varies from committee to committee; oral evidence is almost invariably taken in public, and published, although it will not be available until some time after it was taken; the committees deliberate in private, and their proceedings can be extremely informal.

Although all Select Committees share these characteristics, they function in radically different ways. The domestic committees and the Committee on Finance and Services look inward; they tend to take little formal evidence, and when they do, their main concern is to investigate the needs of members and the extent to which the services of the House can and do meet those needs. Their recommendations will come to the House as a whole, or to the House of Commons Commission, for decision. Their staff are few, and they have little or no need of specialist advice.

The Select Committees which oversee the work of independent officers vary widely. The Public Accounts Committee, which was established in 1861, deals with the work of the Comptroller and Auditor General, and the National Audit Office (NAO). It has a small staff provided from within the House of Commons, but also draws upon the expertise of the staff of the National Audit Office. It takes evidence on each NAO report. The Select Committee to consider the work of the Parliamentary Commissioner for Administration (PCA) has recently been merged with the Public Service Committee to become the Select Committee on Public Administration. The PCA examined the work of the parliamentary ombudsman, encouraging departments and parts of the National Health Service to comply with their recommendations; the new committee, is likely to combine these functions with a broader role (more akin to one of the departmental Select Committees) in considering issues relating to the civil service and the quality and standards of government administration.

The House has also appointed a new independent officer by Standing Order, rather than by statute – the Parliamentary Commissioner for

Standards. The Commissioner has the power to investigate complaints about a member's conduct; his reports are then considered by the Select Committee on Standards and Privileges, and published with their reports.

The Select Committees with legislative functions (the Joint and Select Committees on Statutory Instruments, the Deregulation Committee and the European Legislation Committee) each have a specialist role in considering the technical, and in some cases, political importance of the instruments they consider. They perform a first stage of scrutiny after which matters may be further considered by the House. Affirmative (and controversial negative) Statutory Instruments will then be dealt with by Standing Committees or, in exceptional cases, by the House itself; European Community documents may be recommended for debate either in one of the Standing Committees on European Legislation or on the floor of the House; deregulation Orders are decided by the House itself, without debate if the Deregulation Committee is unanimously agreed that they should be approved, with debate if the committee is divided or recommends the proposal should be amended or rejected. These committees take a great deal of evidence from government departments, and have specialist legal assistance.

The largest, and most prominent group of committees are the departmentally related Select Committees. Their remit is to examine the 'expenditure, administration and policy' of the government departments which they shadow. They are assisted by a small secretariat from within the service of the House: the largest committees may have two clerks, two specialist assistants, and two senior support staff, while the smallest have a clerk and two support staff. The staffing of these committees has been a matter of debate; while outside commentators have remarked on the disparity between the staff of the Select Committees and the government departments that they are expected to monitor, members have been less concerned about this. In 1990, the Procedure Committee agreed with the fear expressed by Sir Ian Lloyd MP that, 'if we had more staff, our inquiries might become staff driven rather than being member driven', and this sentiment was echoed in a report from the Liaison Committee published early this year.[4] However, the House of Commons Commission has recently agreed to increase the complement of Specialist Assistants, to ensure that such staff can be recruited without delay when there is a need for them. In addition to the staff provided by the House, departmental Select Committees make liberal use of the power to appoint specialist advisers, independent experts who provide advice on a 'freelance' basis for modest fees. In the financial year 1995–96, some £187,000 was spent on such advice.

4 Second Report from the Procedure Committee, *The Working of the Select Committee System*, HC (1989–90) 19-I, para 93. First Report from the Liaison Committee, *The Work of Select Committees*, HC (1996–97) 323-I paras 20–21.

Departmental Select Committees choose their own subjects for inquiry, and set their own terms of reference. Sometimes, a committee will monitor the development of a policy over several sessions; between 1987 and 1991 the former Treasury and Civil Service Committee conducted annual inquiries into the devolution of central civil service responsibilities into Next Steps Agencies;[5] sometimes, single inquiries will be directly provoked by the department's policy; for example, in 1992, the Trade and Industry Committee inquired into *British Energy Policy and the Market for Coal*,[6] an inquiry prompted by the announcement of large scale closure of coal mines. Inquiries may be short and technical such as the same Committee's work on *Aspects of the Electricity Supply Industry*.[7] They can be prompted by public concern, such as the Foreign Affairs Committee's inquiry into *Public Expenditure: the Pergau Hydro-electric Project, Malaysia, the Aid and Trade Provision and related matters*.[8] However, Select Committees are not tied to a departmental agenda; they can do what departments perhaps should, but all too often find they cannot do, and take on broad subjects. One example of such an inquiry might be the Public Service Committee's inquiry into Ministerial Accountability and Responsibility.[9]

There is always a tension in any committee between members' roles as part of a body whose function is to subject the legislative proposals, the policies or the actions of the executive to scrutiny, and their roles as members of political parties. The ability of committees to fulfil their functions when their membership reflects party representation in the House as a whole has been doubted, and these doubts are being more urgently expressed now that the governing party has a large, rather than a narrow, majority. However, as the House has reduced the ability of individual members to initiate proceedings, the influence of committees has been increased, and there is no sign that it will decrease. As we have seen, departmental Select Committees have been able to adapt their remits to serve a variety of purposes. New hybrid forms have emerged to improve the ability of committees to scrutinise the executive; a European Standing Committee will hear a statement and question ministers upon it for up to an hour before proceeding to debate the document before it in what used to be the usual fashion; the merging of the PCA and the Public Service Committee should strengthen the House's ability to identify and comment upon any trends in public administration. A Joint Committee is to consider the whole issue of Parliamentary privilege.

5 *Civil Service Management Reform: The Next Steps*, HC (1987–88) 494; *Developments in the Next Steps Programme*, HC (1988–89) 348; *Progress in the Next Steps Initiative*, HC (1989–90) 481; *The Next Steps Initiative*, HC (1990–91) 496.

6 First Report of Session, HC (1992–93) 237.

7 Eleventh Report of Session, HC (1994–95) 481-I.

8 Third Report Session, HC (1993–94) 271-I.

9 Second Report of Session, HC (1995–96) 313A.

We may be at the beginning of a period of extremely rapid evolution; before the end of the last Parliament the Procedure Committee recommended the Select Committees should play a greater part in considering delegated legislation, and there have been calls for greater use to be made of special Standing Committees, committees appointed to consider a Bill but which have power to take evidence for up to three morning sessions, and to meet for a further morning session. The Select Committee on the Modernisation of the House is considering these proposals.

CHAPTER 23

THE FUTURE OF SELECT COMMITTEES

Giles Radice, MP, United Kingdom

The system of departmental Select Committees in the UK Parliament was established, following the report of a Select Committee in 1977–78 (of which I was a member), by the Conservative government in 1979. Opening the debate on the report, the then leader of the House of Commons, Norman St John Stevas, said that this change was 'The most important parliamentary reform of the century', intended 'to redress the balance of power to enable the House of Commons to do more effectively the job it has been elected to do'.

St John Stevas' claim was somewhat over the top. In a parliamentary system backed by a strong party political structure, one cannot expect Select Committees to behave like American Congressional Committees. All the same, over the last two decades, the departmental Select Committees, despite varying performance, have firmly established themselves. Back-benchers are eager to serve on them. Their activities are televised and frequently commented on in the media. Most important of all, ministers and civil servants are now expected on a regular basis to justify themselves and the work and policies of their departments in response to detailed and often sustained questioning by committee members. One unbiased and, in my view, accurate assessment of their record is that they are now 'widely accepted as a legitimate and valued extension of the armoury of back bench scrutiny'.

With the election of a Labour government with an overwhelming majority, the question is whether these departmental committees should now be strengthened. I believe there is a strong case for reform. It is not so much a case, as some commentators have suggested, of select committees providing the real opposition to an over mighty executive. In the British system, one cannot and indeed should not expect Select Committees, with their built-in government majority, to spend their time attacking their own government. They can, however, hold government to account – and it is right and proper to help them carry out that function more effectively.

There are a number of proposals which I would like the Select Committee on the Modernisation of the House to consider. These include the following:

(a) extension of the remit of departmental committees into legislation, especially at the draft stage;

(b) more detailed supervision of devolved agencies which now cover 75% of the civil service; this may require more effective co-operation between departmental committees and the National Audit Office;

(c) greater powers 'to send for persons and papers', so that ministers and civil servants cannot refuse to appear before Select Committees nor departments refuse to supply documents on request;

(d) enhanced status of chairman of committees, in order to help build up the authority of Select Committees;

(e) increase in numbers of staff and specialist advisers;

(f) more prompt governmental responses to Select Committee reports, which should be normally followed by debate.

I remain a strong supporter of the departmental Select Committee system and believe that, backed by sensible reform, they could play an even more important role in making the executive accountable to Parliament.

CHAPTER 24

THE COMMITTEE SYSTEM IN INDIA

Jaswant Singh, MP, India

INTRODUCTION

In a parliamentary polity, the legislature embodies the will of the people. It must, therefore, be able to oversee the way in which public policy is carried out so as to ensure that it keeps in tune with the objectives of socio-economic progress, efficient administration and the aspirations of the people as a whole. This, in a nutshell, is the *raison d' être* of legislative surveillance of the administration. Various procedural devices like the system of committees, Questions, Adjournment Motions, Calling Attention Notices, Half-an-Hour Discussions, etc, through which the legislature becomes informed, constitute very potent instruments for effecting legislative surveillance over administrative actions. In this respect, Parliamentary Committees have come to play a major role in modern parliamentary systems as a means of ensuring executive accountability and transparency in the administration. The phenomenal proliferation of governmental activities has made the task of Parliament very complex and diversified. By its very nature, Parliament as a body cannot have complete control over the government and the whole gamut of its activities. Modern legislatures, therefore, have created, apart from other devices, a system of committees through which they strive to achieve effective surveillance over the administration.

In India, as in other modern democracies, a good deal of the business of Parliament is actually transacted in the committees. Both Houses of Parliament have similar committee structures, with a few exceptions. Their appointments, terms of office, functions and procedure for conducting the business are also similar and are regulated under the provisions of the Rules made by the two Houses under Art 118 (1) of the Constitution.

Broadly speaking, there are two types of Parliamentary Committees, viz: (i) Standing Committees; and (ii) *ad hoc* committees. Standing Committees are elected by the House or nominated by the Speaker (Lok Sabha, the lower House)/Chairman (Rajya Sabha, the upper House) every year or from time to time, as the case may be, and are permanent in nature, whereas *ad hoc* committees are constituted by the House or by the Speaker/Chairman, to consider and report on specific matters and become *functus officio* as soon as they have completed their work.

STANDING COMMITTEES

Among the Standing Committees, the three Financial Committees – Committees on Estimates; Public Accounts; and Public Undertakings – constitute a distinct group as they keep an unremitting vigil over government spending and performance. While members of the Rajya Sabha are associated with the Committees on Public Accounts and Public Undertakings, the members of the Committee on Estimates are drawn entirely from the Lok Sabha. The control exercised by these committees is of a continuous nature. They gather information through questionnaires, memoranda from representative non-official organizations and knowledgeable individuals, on-the-spot studies of organizations and oral examination of official and non-official witnesses. Between them, the Financial Committees examine and report on a fairly large area of the activities of the Union government.

These committees have adequate procedures to ensure that their recommendations are given due consideration by the government. The progress of the implementation of their recommendations as well as any unresolved differences between the committees and the government are set out in the 'Action Taken Reports' which are presented to the House from time to time.

OTHER STANDING COMMITTEES

Other Standing Committees, in each House, divided in terms of their functions, are:

(1) Committees to Inquire:

- (a) the Committee on Petitions examines petitions on Bills and on matters of general public interest and also entertains representations on matters concerning subjects in the Union List; and
- (b) the Committee of Privileges examines any question of privilege referred to it by the House or the Presiding Officer.

(2) Committees to scrutinise:

- (a) the Committee on Government Assurances keeps track of all the assurances, promises, undertakings, etc, given by ministers in the House and pursues them till they are implemented;
- (b) the Committee on Subordinate Legislation scrutinises and reports to the House whether the powers to make regulations, rules, sub-rules, bye-law, etc, conferred by the Constitution or statutes, are being properly exercised by the authorities so authorised; and
- (c) the Committee on Papers Laid on the Table examines all papers

laid on the Table of the House by ministers, other than statutory notifications and orders, which come within the purview of the Committee on Subordinate Legislation, to see whether there has been full compliance with the provisions of the constitution, act, rule or regulation under which the paper has been laid.

(3) Committees relating to the day to day business of the House:

(a) the Business Advisory Committee recommends allocation of time for items of government and other business to be brought before the House;

(b) the Committee on Private Members' Bills and Resolutions of the Lok Sabha classifies and allocates time to Bills introduced by Private Members, recommends allocation of time for discussion on Private Members' resolutions and examines Constitution Amendment Bills before their introduction by Private Members in the Lok Sabha.

The Rajya Sabha, however, does not have such a committee. It is the Business Advisory Committee of that House which recommends the allocation of time for the discussion of stage or stages of Private Members' Bills and resolutions;

(c) the Rules Committee considers matters of procedure and conduct of business in the House and recommends amendments or additions to the rules; and

(d) the Committee on Absence of Members from the Sittings of the House of the Lok Sabha considers all applications from members for leave of absence from the sittings of the House. However, the Rajya Sabha does not have such a committee. Such cases are processed in the Secretariat and an announcement is made to the House.

(4) Committees concerned with the provision of facilities to members:

(a) the General Purposes Committee considers and advises the Speaker/Chairman on matters concerning the affairs of the House, which do not appropriately fall within the purview of any other Parliamentary Committee; and

(b) the House Committee deals with the residential accommodation and other amenities for members.

(v) Joint Committees:

(a) The Committee on the Welfare of Scheduled Castes and Scheduled Tribes, on which members from both Houses serve, considers all matters relating to the welfare of the Scheduled Castes and Scheduled Tribes which come within the purview of the Union government. It also keeps a watch to ensure that constitutional safeguards in respect of these classes are properly implemented;

(b) the Joint Committee on Salaries and Allowances of Members of Parliament is constituted under the Salary, Allowances and Pension of Members of Parliament Act 1954. Apart from framing rules for regulating payment of salary, allowances and pension of members of Parliament, the committee also frames rules in respect of amenities like medical, housing, telephone, postal, constituency and secretarial facilities;

(c) the Joint Committee on Offices of Profit examines the competition and character of the committees and other bodies appointed by the Union and State Governments and Union Territories' Administrations and recommends what offices ought to disqualify their holders from being a member of either House of Parliament; and

(d) the Library Committee consisting of members from both Houses, considers matters concerning the Library of Parliament.

AD HOC COMMITTEES

The *ad hoc* committees may broadly be put into two categories: (i) the Select or Joint Committees on Bills which are appointed to consider and report on particular Bills; and (ii) committees which are constituted to inquire into and report on a specific subject.

INNOVATIONS IN THE COMMITTEE SYSTEM

The Parliament of India has, over the years, introduced several innovations in the committee system. The Business Advisory Committee, Committee on Government Assurances, Committee on Papers Laid on the Table and Committee on the Welfare of Scheduled Castes and Scheduled Tribes, are unique in the Indian parliamentary set up. The system has been further strengthened with the introduction of Departmentally Related Standing Committees on the pattern of UK and other advance democracies.

DEPARTMENTALLY RELATED STANDING COMMITTEES

The most significant recent development has been the appointment of Departmentally Related Specialised Standing Committees of the legislature covering the entire spectrum of administration for an in-depth and continuous study.

The need for a detailed pre-voting scrutiny of the Demands for Grants had, all along, been felt in various parliamentary fora, but the idea of appointing committees for this purpose remained dormant for years. It was only in the late 1970s that the idea of Subject Committees was given serious consideration at various levels.

In 1980, 10 subject based committees were set up by the Kerala Legislature as a sequel to the unanimous recommendations of the All-Parties Committee set up by the Speaker in the Kerala Legislative Assembly in 1979. Though each committee was assigned a fairly well defined subject area, the main functions of all these committees were, *inter alia*, to scrutinise the Demands for Grants, to examine legislation and to consider the draft of rules to be framed by government or other authorities in pursuance of the rule making powers delegated by an Act of the legislature.

Insofar as Parliament is concerned, a beginning was made on 18 August 1989 when Parliament constituted three Subject Committees, one each on Agriculture, Science and Technology and Environment and Forests. The scope of functioning of these three committees was quite wide. The committees functioned under the following broad parameters:

(a) to examine such of the activities of these ministries and allied ministries as may seem fit to the committee;

(b) to report what economies, improvements in organization, efficiency or administrative reforms consistent with the policy approved by Parliament, may be effected;

(c) to examine the Annual Reports of these ministries and allied ministries with a view to finding out whether the expenditure incurred was commensurate with the results achieved;

(d) to examine such of the plan projects/activities of these ministries and allied ministries as may seem fit to the committee or are specially referred to it by the House or the Speaker;

(e) to study the policies and programmes of the government concerning these ministries, etc.

The functioning of these three committees for over three years proved their utility as viable instruments to ensure proper legislative scrutiny over the activities of various departments of the government. There was a general consensus among all concerned that the Parliament should go in for a full fledged system of Departmentally Related Parliamentary Standing Committees. The Speaker of the Lok Sabha took the initiative and discussions were held with the Prime Minister, Leaders of parties, members and others. Thereafter, the agreed proposals were placed before the Rules Committee of the Lok Sabha. Finally, the Rules Committee, in its third report, presented to the Lok Sabha on 29 March 1993, recommended the setting up of 17 Departmentally Related Standing Committees of Parliament. The Rules

Committee of the Lok Sabha also adopted the same report which was presented to the Rajya Sabha on 29 March 1993. Both Houses adopted the report the same day.

Soon thereafter, 17 Departmentally Related Standing Committees were constituted. Out of these, 11 are under the domain of Lok Sabha and six under the Rajya Sabha. The Committees on Agriculture, Communications, Defence, Energy, External Affairs, Finance, Food, Civil Supplies and Public Distribution, Labour and Welfare, Petroleum and Chemicals, Railways and Urban and Rural Development are serviced by the Lok Sabha Secretariat, while the Committees on Commerce, Home Affairs, Human Resource Development, Industry, Science and Technology, Environment and Forests and Transport and Tourism are serviced by the Rajya Sabha Secretariat.

Each committee consists of 45 members. Thirty members from the Lok Sabha are nominated by the Speaker and the remaining 15 members from the Rajya Sabha are nominated by the Chairman.

Ministers are not nominated as members of the committee and if a member, after his nomination to a committee is appointed a minister he ceases to be a member of the committee from the date of such appointment.

The chairman of a committee is appointed by the Chairman of the Rajya Sabha/Speaker of the Lok Sabha from amongst the members of the committee. The term of the committee is one year.

Under the rules, these Standing Committees consider: (i) the Demands for Grants of the concerned ministries and report to the House; (ii) such Bills pertaining to the concerned ministries as are referred to them by the Speaker/Chairman and make report thereon to the House; (iii) basic long term policy documents referred to them by the Speaker/Chairman and report thereon to the House; (iv) the annual reports of the ministries/departments under their purview and the reports on the implementation of the policies and make observations/comments thereon to the House; and (v) other matters of the concerned Ministries referred to them by the Speaker/Chairman.

As regards consideration of the Demands for Grants, the procedure to be followed by the Standing Committees is as follows:

(a) after the General Discussion on the Budget in the House is over, the House adjourns for a month;

(b) the committees consider the Demands for Grants of the ministries concerned during one month's recess of the House;

(c) the committees make their reports within one month and do not ask for more time;

(d) the Demands for Grants are considered by the House in the light of the reports of the committees;

(e) where the reports are required to be made on the basis of votes given by the members in the committees, because of the constitutional provisions, the members of the Lok Sabha in the committee only have the right to vote; and

(f) there is a separate report on the Demands for Grants of each ministry.

The procedure to be followed by the committees in examining Bills is as follows:

(a) after the general principles underlying a Bill have been considered by the House, the committees consider the general principles and the clauses of the Bills and make their report to the House;
(b) consideration of the clauses of the Bill is done by the House in the light of the reports submitted by the committees;
(c) the committees consider only those Bills introduced in the House which were referred to them by the Speaker/Chairman as the case may be;
(d) the committees do not consider the Finance Bills and the Appropriation Bills;
(e) with the permission of the Speaker, urgent Bills may be considered and passed by the House without being considered by the committee; and
(f) the committees are required to make reports on the Bills in the shortest possible time.

The committees may avail themselves of expert opinion or public opinion to make the reports. The reports of the Standing Committees have persuasive value and are treated as considered advice given to the government.

The new committee system represents a ground-breaking endeavour in the area of parliamentary surveillance of the administration. With the emphasis on their functioning on long term plans and policies, these committees provide necessary direction, guidance and inputs for broad policy formulation and achievement of the long term national perspective by the executive.

CONCLUSION

The committee system serves as the arms of the legislature or as an instrument in its hands to make its functioning more effective. A good committee system exists at the heart of legislative process and accountability of the government resides therein. Given the unprecedented growth in the range, magnitude and complexity of governmental activities, legislatures are faced with many complex issues. Constituted as they are, they have neither the time for a thorough scrutiny of varied and complex details of modern administration nor the expertise needed for the task. As a matter of fact, their very size is a handicap. With the increasing business and expanding functions of modern Parliaments, resort to some system of committees has become inevitable in almost all Parliaments of the world. This system facilitates the consideration of issues, consideration which is not possible for the House as a whole. It also results in saving the time of the legislature which could be better utilised for discussion on major issues and matters of policy. The committees help the legislatures to carry out their responsibilities with efficiency and speed. Moreover, the committee atmosphere is more suited for in-depth and non-partisan examination of matters by members having special interest/expertise in the subject matter, away from the glare of publicity. Accommodation of differing points of view and compromises through give and take are more easily achieved in the committees than in the Whole House. Parliamentary government is in fact government by the committees which, apart from serving as instruments of legislative control and surveillance over the executive actions, enables members to have a glimpse of the working of various government agencies/departments and appreciate various problems and constraints faced by them as also the limitations subject to which they have to exercise their authority.

CHAPTER 25

THE FUTURE OF THE COMMITTEE SYSTEM

Jaswant Singh, MP, India

WITH MODERN TELECOMMUNICATIONS, IS A COMMITTEE STRUCTURE NECESSARY OR CAN GOVERNMENT COMMUNICATE WITH THE PUBLIC DIRECTLY?

Though there have been tremendous advancements in the field of telecommunications and information management, the very nature and scope of the committee system do not provide any substitute for it. Committees basically examine issues in detail, study the matter from various angles, call evidence from the people who are concerned with the issues and arrive at independent and objective opinion; subsequently, a report is made and it is presented to the House. The committees perform a useful and objective study of a specific issue on behalf of the entire House and in the process, help save a lot of time of the House. With the help of modern telecommunication facilities, governments can directly communicate with the people and, to some extent, this is happening in many countries. Now, parliamentary proceedings and other important events are available to the public live through the television network. Since the purpose of the committee is totally different, there cannot be any alternative to the work of the committees. A committee has to study an issue systematically and bring out the facts before the House. Merely communicating with the public may not be sufficient as far as committee work is concerned. In many democratic countries, modern electronic gadgets have already reached the Chamber of the Parliament and people are in a position to watch the proceedings in an unrestricted manner. The proceedings of the committees are open to the public and the Press in the United States but, beyond this communication function, committees play a very positive and important role in the American system of governance. Hence, whatever the advancements in the field of communications, the committee system will per force have to continue. The committees could, however, venture to improve their functions with the help of the technology

WILL THE COMMITTEE STRUCTURE CONTINUE TO EVOLVE OR IS IT STATIC?

The committee structure, like the parliamentary system of governance, is a continuously evolving and emerging phenomenon. The role and functioning as well as the area of its operations have been ever evolving and over a period of time the committees have come to play a major role in the democratic system. In all the major democracies, the committees have been able to play a very important role. All the important legislative proposals go through the committee stage before they are finally adopted by the House. In fact, it is at the stage of the committee that all aspects of a Bill are discussed threadbare with the report reflecting on diverse aspects of the legislation. Hence committees have been able to carve out an important position for themselves in the democratic system. It has never been static and with the passage of time the number of the reports produced, the volume of work, etc, of the committees have been increasing. This is an indication of the fact that the committee structure and the system as such are not static.

In India, from 1993 onwards, Departmentally Related Standing Committees have been functioning. There are 17 Departmentally Related Standing Committees, which cover almost all the departments of the governments. Each committee consists of 45 members, 30 members from the Lok Sabha and 15 members from the Rajya Sabha. The functions of these committees are: (a) to consider the Demands for Grants of the concerned ministry/department and make a report on the same to the House; (b) to examine such Bills pertaining to the concerned ministries/departments as are referred to the committee by the chairman of the Rajya Sabha or the Speaker of the Lok Sabha as the case may be and make reports thereon; (c) to consider the annual report of ministries/departments and make reports thereon; and (d) to consider national basic long term policy documents presented to the House if they are referred to the committee by the Chairman or the Speaker and make reports thereon.

Hence, it can be seen that, in the recent times, in the Indian context, the scope of the committee system has expanded enormously. These committees are in addition to the Financial Committees like the PAC, PUC and the Estimates Committee. Besides, there are other joint *ad hoc* committees which are set up to study/examine specific issues and make reports to the House.

Hence, we can see that the committee system has been an ever evolving phenomenon in the Indian context.

Effectiveness of the committee system

It is very often asked whether the committee system is effective. In fact, effectiveness of the committee system can only be gauged from the response the committee reports generate from the various sources like the government, the Press and the public.

Very often, government gives an Action Taken Report on the recommendations of the committee, which is also presented to the House. A majority of the recommendations of the committees are ordinarily accepted by the government and wherever there are difficulties in implementing the recommendations, the position is explained. This is definitely indicative of the fact that the reports of the Parliamentary Committees are effective and the committees are increasingly playing a pivotal role in making the government machinery more responsive and accountable to the public.

Though committees do not have any power in the form of a cut in the budget, etc, and the reports have only persuasive value, still the reports of the Parliamentary Committees often get the required attention from various quarters. Hence, we can definitely say that the committee system is effective and it can be made more effective by bringing in more professionalism in the working of the committees. At present, the committee proceedings in India are not open to the Press and the public, unlike in the United States. Some are of the view that it the committee proceedings are made public, people would come to know more about the actual working of the committees. It would also help in making the public understand how the Parliament works through the system of committees.

Improvements in the system of the committees can be made by various means. Various short term and long term measures could be taken to make the committees more effective. For example, appointment of members to the committees may be made depending on their aptitude, interests and expertise. Members of Parliament come from different walks of life and they may be Doctors, Engineers, Professionals, Advocates, Teachers, Agriculturists, etc. Their professional experience and interests can be considered while making appointments with a view to ensuring that their expertise could be available to the committees.

Ordinarily, the term of the committee is one year. It would be helpful if some members are allowed to continue in the same committee so that they gain enough experience to deal with issues.

It is also essential to provide adequate research and reference input to the committees. Since committee members are also members of Parliament, who have many other parliamentary, constituency and party work to attend, time is very limited. Hence, to provide basic, up-to-date and objective information to the committees, it may be desirable to have a separate research and reference team attached to each committee. They would be able to provide all the reading material/briefs and other information for the use of the committee members for discussing the issues in the committees as well as in the House. The input provided by the research team would be helpful in formulating the committee report in a proper perspective. It is also essential to provide enough support staff for the committees.

WHAT IS THE FUTURE OF THE COMMITTEE SYSTEM? WILL FEATURES OF CONGRESSIONAL COMMITTEE SYSTEM BE INCORPORATED INTO PARLIAMENTARY COMMITTEE STRUCTURE?

Since the committee system has come to stay as one of the most effective and useful methods available to Parliament to ensure executive accountability, there is no doubt that it is not only going to stay but it is going to play an increasingly important role. The phenomenal proliferation of governmental activities has made the task of Parliament and its committees very complex. By its very nature, Parliament as a body cannot have complete control over the government and the whole gamut of its activities. Modern legislatures have, therefore, created a system of committees through which they strive to achieve effective surveillance over the administration.

Whether the features of the Congressional Committee system can be incorporated in to the Parliamentary Committee system in an important question to be seen in the background of the respective systems in operation. The power of the committees vary from Parliament to Parliament. In the United States, the Congressional Committees have considerable scope for independent action. But, under the Westminster system, the committees' scope of operation is limited to making reports and recommendations to the House. In most Parliaments, committees operate as a component part of the parent House. By contrast, the US Congressional Committees operate to a great extent as self-contained entities with a wide measure of independence. Both Houses of the Congress appoint a range of Standing Committees. The fate of legislation is largely determined by these committees. It is difficult and some times impossible to overcome the objections of a committee which in determined to block the progress of a Bill. In practice, it is the committees which control the legislative agenda as Congress usually deals only with those Bills which have been reported from committees. Congressional Committees, have in fact been described as 'little legislatures' in recognition of the extent to which Congress has surrendered its initiative to its committees. Standing Committees are also mandated to oversee the government departments and agencies falling within the scope of their respective responsibilities and their unlimited powers of investigation further augment their influence.

The committee chairmen, and many subcommittee chairmen as well, are powerful figures in the American Congressional system. Chairmanship of both the committees and subcommittees belong as of right to the majority party in the House concerned. The Chairman calls the meetings, establishes the agenda, arranges hearings, controls the funds and staff of the committee and gives general direction to its activities.

The congress also appoints Special Committees and Joint Committees which usually have investigative, rather than legislative, functions.

From the foregoing analysis, it is clear that the US Congressional Committees are different from the Parliamentary Committees. However, in terms of broad framework and role and functions, all Parliamentary Committees do more or less the same work. The difference is only in the powers vested with the committee, that too in a limited sense.

In India, too, the chairman has the power to call for evidence, records and officers. The reports are presented to the House which has the ultimate power to act upon it. In India, also, the reports of the committees are given due weightage before a Bill is passed. In fact, the House gives due recognition to the opinion of the committee though these reports have only persuasive value. committees like Parliaments, are dynamic mechanisms. They keep evolving all the time, coping with emerging realities. The ultimate purpose of the committee is to ensure executive accountability to the legislature – be it in the US congressional set up on in a parliamentary set up.